SOURCE READINGS IN $\mathcal{M}$USIC HISTORY

SOURCE READINGS IN *Music* HISTORY

OLIVER STRUNK

EDITOR

Revised Edition

LEO TREITLER GENERAL EDITOR

VOLUME 2

The Early Christian Period and the Latin Middle Ages

Edited by JAMES McKINNON

 W · W · NORTON & COMPANY

New York · London

The text of this book is composed in Caledonia
with the display set in Bauer Bodoni and Optima.
Composition by the Maple-Vail Book Manufacturing Group
Manufacturing by Maple-Vail Book Manufacturing Group
Book design by Jack Meserole
Cover illustration by Mary Frank

The Library of Congress has cataloged the one-volume edition as follows:

Source readings in music history / Oliver Strunk, editor. — Rev. ed.
    / Leo Treitler, general editor.
        p.   cm.
    Also published in a 7 v. ed.
    Includes bibliographical references and index.
    ISBN 0-393-03752-5
    1. Music—History and criticism—Sources.   I. Strunk, W. Oliver
(William Oliver), 1901–   . II. Treitler, Leo, 1931–   .
ML160.S89   1998
780′.9—dc20   94-34569
                                                       MN

ISBN 0-393-96695-X (pbk.)

W. W. Norton & Company, Inc., 500 Fifth Avenue, New York, N.Y. 10110
http://www.wwnorton.com

W. W. Norton & Company Ltd., 10 Coptic Street, London WC1A 1PU

1 2 3 4 5 6 7 8 9 0

FROM THE FOREWORD TO THE FIRST EDITION OF *SOURCE READINGS IN MUSIC HISTORY*

*T*his book began as an attempt to carry out a suggestion made in 1929 by Carl Engel in his "Views and Reviews"—to fulfil his wish for "a living record of musical personalities, events, conditions, tastes . . . a history of music faithfully and entirely carved from contemporary accounts."[1] It owes something, too, to the well-known compilations of Kinsky[2] and Schering[3] and rather more, perhaps, to Andrea della Corte's *Antologia della storia della musica*[4] and to an evaluation of this, its first model, by Alfred Einstein.

In its present form, however, it is neither the book that Engel asked for nor a literary anthology precisely comparable to the pictorial and musical ones of Kinsky and Schering, still less an English version of its Italian predecessor, with which it no longer has much in common. It departs from Engel's ideal scheme in that it has, at bottom, a practical purpose—to make conveniently accessible to the teacher or student of the history of music those things which he must eventually read. Historical documents being what they are, it inevitably lacks the seemingly unbroken continuity of Kinsky and Schering; at the same time, and for the same reason, it contains far more that is unique and irreplaceable than either of these. Unlike della Corte's book it restricts itself to historical documents as such, excluding the writing of present-day historians; aside from this, it naturally includes more translations, fewer original documents, and while recognizing that the somewhat limited scope of the *Antologia* was wholly appropriate in a book on music addressed to Italian readers, it seeks to take a broader view.

That, at certain moments in its development, music has been a subject of widespread and lively contemporary interest, calling forth a flood of documentation, while at other moments, perhaps not less critical, the records are either silent or unrevealing—this is in no way remarkable, for it is inherent in the very nature of music, of letters, and of history. The beginnings of the Classical

1. *The Musical Quarterly* 15, no. 2 (April 1929): 301.
2. *Geschichte der Musik in Bildern* (Leipzig, 1929; English edition by E. Blom, London, 1930).
3. *Geschichte der Musik in Beispielen* (Leipzig, 1931; English edition New York, 1950).
4. Two volumes (Torino, 1929). Under the title *Antologia della storia della musica della Grecia antica al' ottocento*, one volume (Torino, 1945).

symphony and string quartet passed virtually unnoticed as developments without interest for the literary man; the beginnings of the opera and cantata, developments which concerned him immediately and deeply, were heralded and
reviewed in documents so numerous that, even in a book of this size, it has
been possible to include only the most significant. Thus, as already suggested,
a documentary history of music cannot properly exhibit even the degree of
continuity that is possible for an iconographic one or a collection of musical
monuments, still less the degree expected of an interpretation. For this reason,
too, I have rejected the simple chronological arrangement as inappropriate and
misleading and have preferred to allow the documents to arrange themselves
naturally under the various topics chronologically ordered in the table of contents and the book itself, some of these admirably precise, others perhaps
rather too inclusive. As Engel shrewdly anticipated, the frieze has turned out
to be incomplete, and I have left the gaps unfilled, as he wished.

For much the same reason, I have not sought to give the book a spurious
unity by imposing upon it a particular point of view. At one time it is the
musician himself who has the most revealing thing to say; at another time he
lets someone else do the talking for him. And even when the musician speaks
it is not always the composer who speaks most clearly; sometimes it is the
theorist, at other times the performer. If this means that few readers will find
the book uniformly interesting, it ought also to mean that "the changing pat-
terns of life," as Engel called them, will be the more fully and the more faithfully reflected. . . . In general, the aim has been to do justice to every age
without giving to any a disproportionate share of the space.

It was never my intention to compile a musical Bartlett, and I have accordingly sought, wherever possible, to include the complete text of the selection
chosen, or—failing this—the complete text of a continuous, self-contained, and
independently intelligible passage or series of passages, with or without regard
for the chapter divisions of the original. But in a few cases I have made cuts to
eliminate digressions or to avoid needless repetitions of things equally well said
by earlier writers; in other cases the excessive length and involved construction
of the original has forced me to abridge, reducing the scale of the whole while
retaining the essential continuity of the argument. All cuts are clearly indicated,
either by a row of dots or in annotations.

Often, in the course of my reading, I have run across memorable things said
by writers on music which, for one reason or another, were not suited for
inclusion in the body of this book. One of these, however, is eminently suited
for inclusion here. It is by Thomas Morley, and it reads as follows:

> But as concerning the book itself, if I had, before I began it, imagined half the pains
> and labor which it cost me, I would sooner have been persuaded to anything than to
> have taken in hand such a tedious piece of work, like unto a great sea, which the
> further I entered into, the more I saw before me unpassed; so that at length, despair-
> ing ever to make an end (seeing that grow so big in mine hands which I thought to
> have shut up in two or three sheets of paper), I laid it aside, in full determination to

have proceeded no further but to have left it off as shamefully as it was foolishly begun. But then being admonished by some of my friends that it were pity to lose the fruits of the employment of so many good hours, and how justly I should be condemned of ignorant presumption—in taking that in hand which I could not perform—if I did not go forward, I resolved to endure whatsoever pain, labor, loss of time and expense, and what not, rather than to leave that unbrought to an end in the which I was so far engulfed.[5]

OLIVER STRUNK
The American Academy in Rome

5. Thomas Morley, *A Plain and Easy Introduction to Practical Music,* ed. R. Alec Harman (New York: Norton, 1966), p. 5.

FOREWORD TO THE REVISED EDITION

> *Hiding in the peace of these deserts*
> *with few but wise books bound together*
> *I live in conversation with the departed,*
> *and listen with my eyes to the dead.*
>   —*Francisco Gómez de Quevedo*
>   *(1580–1645)*

The inclusion here of portions of Oliver Strunk's foreword to the original edition of this classic work (to which he habitually referred ironically as his *opus unicum*) is already a kind of exception to his own stricture to collect in it only "historical documents as such, excluding the writing of present-day historians." For his foreword itself, together with the book whose purpose and principles it enunciates and the readings it introduces, comes down to us as a historical document with which this revision is in a conversation—one that ranges over many subjects, even the very nature of music history.

This principle of exclusion worked for Strunk because he stopped his gathering short of the twentieth century, which has been characterized—as Robert Morgan observes in his introduction to the twentieth-century readings in this series—by "a deep-seated self-consciousness about what music is, to whom it should be addressed, and its proper role within the contemporary world." It is hardly possible to segregate historian from historical actor in our century.

For the collection in each of the seven volumes in this series the conversation begins explicitly with an introductory essay by its editor and continues with the readings themselves. The essays provide occasions for the authors to describe the considerations that guide their choices and to reflect on the character of the age in each instance, on the regard in which that age has been held in music-historical tradition, on its place in the panorama of music history as we construct and continually reconstruct it, and on the significance of the readings themselves. These essays constitute in each case the only substantial explicit interventions by the editors. We have otherwise sought to follow Strunk's own essentially conservative guidelines for annotations.

The essays present new perspectives on music history that have much in common, whatever their differences, and they present new perspectives on the music that is associated with the readings. They have implications, therefore, for those concerned with the analysis and theory of music as well as for students of music history. It is recommended that even readers whose interest is focused on one particular age acquaint themselves with all of these essays.

The opportunity presented by this revision to enlarge the book has, of course, made it possible to extend the reach of its contents. Its broader scope reflects achievement since 1950 in research and publication. But it reflects, as well, shifts in the interests and attitudes that guide music scholarship, even changes in intellectual mood in general. That is most immediately evident in the revised taxonomy of musical periods manifest in the new titles for some of the volumes, and it becomes still more evident in the introductory essays. The collections for "Antiquity and the Middle Ages" have been separated and enlarged. What was "The Greek View of Music" has become *Greek Views of Music* (eight of them, writes Thomas J. Mathiesen), and "The Middle Ages" is now, as James McKinnon articulates it, *The Early Christian Period and the Latin Middle Ages.* There is no longer a collection for "The Classical Era" but one for *The Late Eighteenth Century,* and in place of the epithet "The Romantic Era" Ruth Solie has chosen *The Nineteenth Century.* The replacements in the latter two cases represent a questioning of the labels "Classic" and "Romantic," long familiar as tokens for the phases of an era of "common practice" that has been held to constitute the musical present. The historiographic issues that are entailed here are clarified in Solie's and Wye Jamison Allanbrook's introductory essays. And the habit of thought that is in question is, of course, directly challenged as well by the very addition of a collection of readings from the twentieth century, which makes its own claims to speak for the present. Only the labels "Renaissance" and "Baroque" have been retained as period designations. But the former is represented by Gary Tomlinson as an age in fragmentation, for which "Renaissance" is retained only *faute de mieux,* and as to the latter, Margaret Murata places new emphasis on the indeterminate state of its music.

These new vantage points honor—perhaps more sharply than he would have expected—Strunk's own wish "to do justice to every age," to eschew the "spurious unity" of a "particular point of view" and the representation of history as a succession of uniform periods, allowing the music and music-directed thought of *each* age to appear as an "independent phenomenon," as Allanbrook would have us regard the late eighteenth century.

The possibility of including a larger number of readings in this revision might have been thought to hold out the promise of our achieving greater familiarity with each age. But several of the editors have made clear—explicitly or implicitly through their selections—that as we learn more about a culture it seems "more, not less distant and estranged from ours," as Tomlinson writes of the Renaissance. That is hardly surprising. If the appearance of familiarity has arisen out of a tendency to represent the past in our own image, we should hardly wonder that the past sounds foreign to us—at least initially—as we allow it to speak to us more directly in its own voice.

But these words are written as though we would have a clear vision of our image in the late twentieth century, something that hardly takes account of the link, to which Tomlinson draws attention, between the decline of our confidence about historical certainties and the loss of certainty about our own identities. Standing neck-deep in the twentieth century, surrounded by uncountable numbers of voices all speaking at once, the editor of this newest selection of source readings may, ironically, have the most difficult time of any in arriving at a selection that will make a recognizable portrait of the age, as Morgan confesses.

Confronted with a present and past more strange and uncertain than what we have been pleased to think, the editors have not been able to carry on quite in the spirit of Strunk's assuredness about making accessible "those things which [the student] must eventually read." Accordingly, this revision is put forward with no claim for the canonical status of its contents. That aim has necessarily yielded some ground to a wish to bring into the conversation what has heretofore been marginal or altogether silent in accounts of music history.

The sceptical tract *Against the Professors* by Sextus Empiricus, among the readings from ancient Greece, is the first of numerous readings that run against a "mainstream," with the readings gathered under the heading "Music, Magic, Gnosis" in the Renaissance section being perhaps the most striking. The passage from Hildegard's *Epistle* to the prelates of Mainz in the medieval collection is the first of many selections written by women. The readings grouped under the reading "European Awareness of Other Musical Worlds" in the Renaissance collection evince the earliest attention paid to that subject. A new prominence is given to performance and to the reactions of listeners in the collection from the Baroque. And the voices of North American writers and writers of color begin to be heard in the collection from the nineteenth century.

There is need to develop further these once-marginal strands in the representation of Western music history, and to draw in still others, perhaps in some future version of this series, and elsewhere—the musical cultures of Latin America for one example, whose absence is lamented by Murata, and the representation of the Middle Ages in their truly cosmopolitan aspect, for another.

This series of books remains at its core the conception and the work of Oliver Strunk. Its revision is the achievement of the editors of the individual volumes, most of whom have in turn benefited from the advice of numerous colleagues working in their fields of specialization. Participating in such a broadly collaborative venture has been a most gratifying experience, and an encouraging one in a time that is sometimes marked by a certain agonistic temper.

The initiative for this revision came in 1988 from Claire Brook, who was then music editor of W. W. Norton. I am indebted to her for granting me the privilege of organizing it and for our fruitful planning discussions at the outset. Her thoughts about the project are manifested in the outcome in too many ways to enumerate. Her successor Michael Ochs has been a dedicated and active editor, aiming always for the highest standards and expediting with expertise the complex tasks that such a project entails.

Leo Treitler
Lake Hill, New York

CONTENTS

NOTES AND ABBREVIATIONS

Footnotes by the authors of the texts are marked [Au.], those by the translators
[Tr.].

References to other volumes in this series are indicated as follows:

SR   Oliver Strunk, ed., *Source Readings in Music History,* rev. ed., Leo
        Treitler, ed., (New York: W. W. Norton, 1997)

SR 1   Oliver Strunk, ed., *Source Readings in Music History,* rev. ed., Leo
        Treitler, ed., vol. 1: *Greek Views of Music,* Thomas J. Mathiesen,
        ed. (New York: W. W. Norton, 1997)

Years in the common era (A.D.) are indicated as C.E. and those before the
common era as B.C.E.

THE EARLY CHRISTIAN PERIOD AND THE LATIN MIDDLE AGES

INTRODUCTION

The pages that follow provide a representative selection of writings about music from the Early Christian period and from the Latin Middle Ages. The material appears in four sections of markedly different character. The first offers a sampling of passages from the rich literature of the Early Christian Church Fathers. These eminent fourth-century ecclesiastics from East and West—St. John Chrysostom, for example, and St. Augustine—express their views on the singing of psalms. In the second section, Boethius, Cassiodorus, and Isidore of Seville, the principal figures in the transmission of classical culture to the Middle Ages, illustrate the part that music played in that process. The third section provides a series of readings on early medieval ecclesiastical chant and its liturgical context. Included are descriptions of the Mass and the Office and conflicting accounts of an event in the history of Western music that is as puzzling as it is important—the transmission of Roman chant across the Alps to the Carolingian realm. The fourth and longest section is taken up with extended readings, in some cases entire short treatises, from the theoretical and pedagogical literature of the Middle Ages. Several of these selections deal with the development of modal theory, the central problem of earlier medieval musical theory, while others treat the rhythmic theory of thirteenth- and fourteenth-century polyphonic music.

Most of the Early Christian writing on music does not appear in works that are devoted entirely to music, but rather in occasional passages scattered throughout various types of religious literature. Three of the selections translated here represent an exegetical genre popular at the time, the psalm commentary, and another is taken from St. Augustine's celebrated autobiography *The Confessions*. Only one reading is drawn from a work that treats music exclusively, Niceta of Remesiana's unique sermon on *The Benefits of Psalmody*. There are, certainly, a considerable number of writings from the period that deal with music alone. For the most part these are theoretical treatises that explain music as one of the mathematical disciplines of the liberal arts. The authors of these tracts are for the most part pagans, but in the later fourth century, as the society of Late Antiquity comes to be increasingly Christianized, a figure such as St. Augustine can make his own contribution to the genre. His *De Musica* was intended as only one treatise in a series on the seven liberal arts. It deals with the rhythmic and metrical aspect of its subject, leaving the tonal aspect—what the ancients called harmonics—to a second work on music theory that was planned but never written. In the sixth and final book of the treatise, Augustine clothed his subject in the garb of Christian examples, using a hymn text to make his points about rhythm, but the work as a whole remains more a representative of the classical tradition than an exemplar of the Christian view of music.

Musica in Late Antiquity was not so much the everyday product of singing and playing that we call music today as it was the academic enterprise that we call music theory. Moreover, the music theory of the time was considerably more abstract than the effort that goes by that name in recent times; certainly it has little in common with the music theory that explains eighteenth- and nineteenth-century harmonic practice. In Late Antiquity the subject was permeated with Neoplatonic thinking, where ideas were considered to be real and where external manifestations of any sort—what we call reality—were mere shadows of those ideas. In this context the theoretical constructs themselves were the musical reality: good theory was the product of sophisticated mathematical calculation and the ingenious manipulation of tonal symmetries.

If, then, we are to understand the views of Augustine and his contemporaries on everyday music, we must turn from their writings on music as such to other types of literature, where they might have occasion to bring up the subject. In the case of Christian authors, the single genre of literature that speaks most often of music is the psalm commentary, a work in which the writer moves systematically through the 150 psalms, annotating nearly every verse of each one. The predominant style of the genre is the so-called allegorical method of exegesis. In this style the author is more concerned with the spiritual meaning of a passage than its literal or historical meaning. A reference, for example, to the hide that is stretched upon a frame to make a drum will lead the Church Father to comment on the mortification of the flesh rather than on percussive rhythms. Despite the extreme tendency of Late Antique intellectuals toward abstraction, ecclesiastical authors often lapse into remarks about everyday musical reality, even in the midst of a generally allegorical exegesis. To a Church Father, everyday musical reality was two things: the pagan musical practice that surrounded the Christian population on every side and the singing of psalms and hymns in church. The former was the subject of scathing denunciation because of its immoral associations, and the latter was generally approved as a beneficial, if sometimes suspect, practice. This second attitude is well exemplified by the readings presented here.

All three readings of the second section represent *musica* in the proper classical sense rather than music in its everyday sense. We observe the authors—Boethius, Cassiodorus, and Isidore—striving to provide a summary of the classical doctrine on music and doing so entirely without reference to the music of their own day. The example of Boethius is particularly interesting in this respect. We know that he was a Christian theologian who wrote a treatise on the Trinity, yet not once in his lengthy work on music does he mention the ecclesiastical music of his day. Even more remarkable perhaps is that while in prison awaiting execution, he wrote his *On the Consolation of Philosophy* without a single reference to his Christian faith. *Philosophia*, like *musica*, was an academic subject; each existed as a world unto itself, valued as a thing of the mind, and valued moreover because it was a microcosm within the system of classical education.

In the case of music, at least, this sort of intellectual compartmentalization appears to have been of benefit to medieval writers. The digests of classical music theory composed by these transitional authors provided their medieval successors with a theoretical vocabulary that they could apply to the music of their own time—not that Boethius, Cassiodorus, and Isidore thought of themselves as performing such a function (they certainly had no way of imagining their future medieval readership).

On the other hand they might very well have understood their relationship to their present and their past. They lived during what we look on as the twilight of Classical Antiquity. Although the Roman Empire had been swept by waves of barbarian invasion in the fifth century, these figures lived in circumstances of comparative stability. Boethius worked at Ravenna under the relatively benevolent Ostrogothic king Theodoric in earlier sixth-century Italy, and Isidore at Seville lived under similarly benevolent Visigothic sovereigns in earlier seventh-century Spain. The conditions under which Cassiodorus worked were different only in detail. He began his career in the same Ostrogothic court as did Boethius, but lived virtually until the end of the sixth century. He wrote his treatise on music many years after the death of Boethius, while in residence at his monastery of Vivarium in southern Italy. All three authors knew of no civilization other than that of the classical world. In spite of the intrusive barbarian presence, much of the external grandeur of that world—its public buildings, aqueducts, and circuses—was still in evidence, and its rich literature was still available. The literature was taught selectively, however, and to only a dwindling minority of the population. The three writers were surely aware that they represented a greatly weakened tradition, possibly even one in mortal peril. But they had no way of imagining themselves as transitional figures; more likely they saw their role as that of preserving a measure of their intellectual heritage and conveying it to their contemporaries.

The third section takes us to the world of *cantus*, the medieval term for all practical music, although the writings furnished here are confined to ecclesiastical chant and its liturgical context. The first reading presents the portion of St. Benedict's Rule that describes the early medieval monastic Office, that is, the series of eight services that occupied much of a medieval ecclesiastic's waking hours, from well before dawn until dusk. St. Benedict's was not the first monastic rule, but the same masterful clarity and succinctness that characterize his description of the Office are maintained throughout the entire document, contributing greatly to its near universal adoption by Western monasticism in later centuries. Benedict composed his Rule for his newly established community at Monte Cassino in about 530, just a few years after the death of Boethius, and only a few decades before Cassiodorus founded his own monastery at

Vivarium. Unlike Boethius and Cassiodorus, Benedict certainly did not see himself as preserving classical culture. In his youth he had been sent to Rome to further his education and had been appalled by the worldliness of that still impressive capital. But he shares with his Italian contemporaries the role of unwitting founder of medieval society. He designed his rule for his small band of monastic disciples at Monte Cassino, never dreaming that it would become one of the most influential books in the history of Western civilization.

Just as the reading from Benedict's Rule serves as a conveniently compact description of the medieval Office, so the excerpt from *Ordo romanus XVII* serves as a brief, virtually laconic, description of the medieval Mass. The *Exposition of the Ancient Gallican Rite,* however, is a document of different character. Its elaborately allegorical style is anything but compact or laconic, yet a relatively clear description of a Gallican Mass can be extracted from its fanciful symbolic explanation of that rite. At the same time, its very use of the allegorical style vividly exemplifies the method of allegorical exegesis, described above in connection with the Early Christian psalm commentary, that was applied here in the early Middle Ages to a genre different from that of biblical exegesis.

The following three readings deal with one of the central questions in the historiography of medieval music, how the chant fared in its transmission from Rome to the northern realm of the Carolingians. We know certain things about the process, for example, that Pope Stephen II brought Roman singers with him when he visited Pepin the Short in 754, and that the Franks were so impressed by the Roman chant that Pepin decided to replace the indigenous Gallican liturgy with that of the Romans. We also know that the Roman singers brought the texts of the chant in written form—certainly the texts of the Mass chants and quite possibly those of the Office—while the melodies, on the other hand, were somehow transmitted orally. And finally, we know that the melodies achieved a stable form by about 900 at the latest, because we have copies from that time in Frankish manuscripts with musical notation. But that leaves us with an immense gap in our knowledge. How much did the chant melodies change from their original orally transmitted Roman form to their final written Frankish form?

The three readings translated here form an important part of the evidence that scholars use to support their positions on this highly controversial question. The letter of Abbot Helisachar describes his efforts to establish a satisfactory antiphonary of the Office. It provides a sober and authoritative account by a contemporary witness on one important aspect of the transmission process. The passages from John the Deacon's life of Gregory the Great and from the Monk of St. Gall's life of Charlemagne provide sharply contrasting retrospective histories—the former from the Roman point of view and the latter from the Frankish—of how the Roman chant fared during its early years in Francia. Both documents, while entertainingly prejudiced and fanciful in style, are not without a measure of historical truth to be extracted by the careful reader.

The final reading of this section provides a touching and richly allusive passage from the writings of Hildegard of Bingen, in which she describes how her convent has been deprived of the consolation of the sung Office.

In the final section, on medieval music theory and pedagogy, we witness the marriage of *musica* and *cantus*. The Carolingian music theorists took the vocabulary and basic concepts of classical Greek music theory, chiefly as derived from Boethius, and applied them to their contemporary music, the so-called Gregorian chant. In doing so they distorted the original, but this is of little significance. What is important is that they and their successors developed a body of music theory that not only described their musical practice in a consistent and systematic way, but set Western music on its peculiarly rational course. In the earlier centuries of the discipline they rationalized music vertically, so to speak, in developing a theory of musical space—the system of eight ecclesiastical modes placed on a grid of intervals derived from mathematical ratios. And in later centuries, with the emergence of polyphonic music, they rationalized music horizontally with the development of increasingly complex ways of measuring musical duration. This twofold rationalization, to continue the argument, can be looked upon as having had a dual effect on Western classical music. It permitted the eventual composition of great architectonic musical structures like those of the later eighteenth and earlier nineteenth centuries, but it may have forced Western music to sacrifice much of the rhythmic and tonal nuance that characterizes the musics of certain other high cultures.

In any event, the merger of *musica* and *cantus* did take place, and the final section provides a generous selection from the resulting literature of medieval music theory. The first examples show the later Carolingians—in monastery, court, and cathedral—as they struggled to manipulate the Boethian tonal system into one that corresponded to the realities of contemporary ecclesiastical chant. There follows an interlude of inspired pedagogy as the great Guido of Arezzo and his Italian monastic contemporaries succeed admirably in applying the new theory to the task of teaching the chant, most notably with the use of the musical staff. And finally we witness the rapid development of rhythmic systems in the scholastic milieu of thirteenth- and fourteenth-century Paris. The so-called modal rhythm of the *Discantus positio vulgaris* is followed by the mensural rhythm of Franco's *Ars cantus mensurabilis*, which is followed, in turn, by the refinements of the fourteenth-century *ars nova* as summarized in Jehan des Murs's *Notitia artis musicae*, refinements which are then roundly denounced by the arch-conservative Jacques of Liège.

Finally one notes the intrusion of the later thirteenth-century Spanish cleric Aegidius of Zamora into this series of Parisian-based theorists on rhythm. He provides us with a colorful expansion on the medieval topos of the "inventors of music." His choice for the original inventor is the Bible's Jubal, who heard his brother Tubalcain ring out the musical consonances on his blacksmith's anvil. In his view, the Greeks engaged in deceit in claiming that Pythagoras made this discovery while one day passing by a smithy. Aegidius, who wrote on natural history as well as music theory, also describes a series of musical marvels in nature, ranging from the unsurprising musical feats of the nightingale to the somewhat unexpected accomplishments of musical dolphins. The reader will recognize in these tales about the musicians of nature the same impulse that underlies the medieval bestiaries. Indeed this entire selection from the literature on music, ranging from the fourth-century Church Fathers to the fourteenth-century scholastics, can be viewed as a microcosm of medieval literature in general.

*   *   *

I wish to express my gratitude to three scholars who came to my aid in the delicate task of reediting this portion of Oliver Strunk's classic work: Charles Atkinson, Richard Crocker, and Leo Treitler. The last named, especially, in his dual capacities as general editor and distinguished medievalist, gave wise counsel on every aspect of the revision, from details of annotation to the selection of new material. But my greatest debt is to Oliver Strunk himself, both for his original choice of material and for his translations. Even though I found it advisable to modernize the language to some degree—for example, in providing a less Latinate word order—throughout my work I continued to marvel at how he had wrestled the correct sense out of numerous obscure passages. In the choice of readings, his superb judgment remains clear after more than forty years of development in the field of medieval music. While all those I consulted could think of readings to add, there was little indeed from the original that they wished to replace. And in this area of selection I believe that I can claim unique help from Strunk. Some thirty years ago, as a graduate student engaged in the study of patristics and music, I met him and made bold to compliment him on his choice of readings from the Church Fathers. He modestly brushed aside my remarks and reproached himself instead for having omitted the Rule of St. Benedict. Needless to say, the present edition gratefully accepts his advice on this point.

$\mathcal{E}$ARLY CHRISTIAN VIEWS OF MUSIC

1 St. Basil

St. Basil the Great, brother of St. Gregory of Nyssa and St. Macrina, was born at Caesarea, Cappadocia, about 330 C.E. Educated at Constantinople and Athens, he retired after extensive travels to his desert retreat at Pontus, where he wrote the two Rules that came to be influential in the development of eastern monasticism. He was named bishop of Caesarea in 370 and died in 379.

Although an influential opponent of the Arian heresy, he has been called a "Roman among the Greeks" because he is better characterized as a practical churchman than as a speculative theologian. In addition to his efforts to foster monasticism, he was an energetic builder of charitable institutions, an inspired preacher, a prolific writer of letters, and a liturgical innovator.

FROM *Homily on the First Psalm*

1. All scripture is inspired by God and is profitable;[1] it was composed by the Holy Spirit to the end that all we men, as in a common dispensary for souls, might each select the medicine for his own disease. For "medicine," it is said, "causes great offenses to cease."[2] The Prophets therefore teach certain things, the Histories others, the Law others, and the kind of counsel given in the Proverbs others. But the Book of Psalms embraces whatever in all the others is helpful. It prophesies things to come, it recalls histories to the mind, it gives laws for living, it counsels what is to be done. And altogether it is a storehouse of good instructions, diligently providing for each what is useful to him. For it heals the ancient wounds of souls and brings prompt relief to the newly wounded; it ministers to what is sick and preserves what is healthy; and it wholly removes the ills, howsoever great and of whatsoever kind, that attack souls in our human life; and this by means of a certain well-timed persuasion which inspires wholesome reflection.

For when the Holy Spirit saw that mankind was ill-inclined toward virtue and that we were heedless of the righteous life because of our inclination to pleasure, what did he do? He blended the delight of melody with doctrine in order that through the pleasantness and softness of the sound we might unawares receive what was useful in the words, according to the practice of wise physicians, who, when they give the more bitter draughts to the sick, often smear the rim of the cup with honey. For this purpose these harmonious melodies of the Psalms have been designed for us, that those who are of boyish age or wholly youthful in their character, while in appearance they sing, may in reality be educating their souls. For hardly a single one of the many, and

TEXT: Jacques Migne, ed., *Patrologia cursus completus. Series graeca*, vol. 29, cols. 209–13. Translation by William Strunk, Jr., and Oliver Strunk, revised by James McKinnon.

1. 2 Timothy 3:16.
2. Ecclesiastes 10:4.

even of the indolent, has gone away retaining in his memory any precept of the
apostles or of the prophets, but the oracles of the Psalms they both sing at
home and disseminate in the marketplace. And if somewhere one who rages
like a wild beast from excessive anger falls under the spell of the psalm, he
straightway departs, with the fierceness of his soul calmed by the melody.

2. A psalm is the tranquillity of souls, the arbitrator of peace, restraining the
disorder and turbulence of thoughts, for it softens the passion of the soul and
moderates its unruliness. A psalm forms friendships, unites the divided, medi-
ates between enemies. For who can still consider him an enemy with whom he
has sent forth one voice to God? So that the singing of psalms brings love, the
greatest of good things, contriving harmony like some bond of union and unit-
ing the people in the symphony of a single choir.

A psalm drives away demons, summons the help of angels, furnishes arms
against nightly terrors, and gives respite from daily toil; to little children it is
safety, to men in their prime an adornment, to the old a solace, to women their
most fitting ornament. It populates the deserts, it brings agreement to the
marketplaces. To novices it is a beginning; to those who are advancing, an
increase; to those who are concluding, a confirmation. A psalm is the voice of
the Church. It gladdens feast days, it creates the grief which is in accord with
God's will, for a psalm brings a tear even from a heart of stone.

A psalm is the work of the angels, the ordinance of Heaven, the incense of
the Spirit. Oh, the wise invention of the teacher who devised how we might at
the same time sing and learn profitable things, whereby doctrines are somehow
more deeply impressed upon the mind!

What is learned unwillingly does not naturally remain, but things which are
received with pleasure and love fix themselves more firmly in our minds. For
what can we not learn from the Psalms? Can we not learn the splendor of
courage, the exactness of justice, the dignity of self-control, the habit of repen-
tance, the measure of patience, whatsoever good things that you may name?
Here is perfect theology; here is foretold the Incarnation of Christ; here are
the threat of judgment, the hope of resurrection, the fear of punishment, the
assurances of glory, the revelations of mysteries; all things are brought together
in the Book of Psalms as in some great and common storehouse.

Although there are many musical instruments, the prophet made this book
suited to the psaltery, as it is called, revealing, it seems to me, the grace from
on high which sounded in him through the Holy Spirit, since this alone, of all
musical instruments, has the source of its sound above. For the brass wires of
the cithara and the lyre sound from below against the plectrum, but the psaltery has the origins of its harmonious rhythms above, in order that we may
study to seek for those things which are on high and not be drawn down by the
pleasantness of the melody to the passions of the flesh.[3] And I think that by

---

3. This comparison between the psaltery and the cithara is typical of the patristic allegorical exegesis of biblical musical instruments; see James W. McKinnon, "Musical Instruments in Medieval

reason of this structure of the instrument the words of the prophet profoundly and wisely reveal to us that those whose souls are attuned and harmonious have an easy path to things above. But now let us examine the beginning of the Psalms.

Psalm Commentaries and Psalters," *Journal of the American Musicological Society* 21 (1968), especially pp. 4–13.

2 St. John Chrysostom

St. John, born to a wealthy family in Antioch about 345 C.E., was thoroughly educated in rhetoric under the renowned teacher Libanius. A longtime admirer of the monastic life, he left the home of his widowed mother about 373 to live a life of severe privation as a hermit. With his health permanently impaired, he returned to Antioch to serve as deacon from 381 and then as priest from 386 to 398, the period when he delivered the bulk of his famous homilies.

In 398 he reluctantly consented to consecration as Patriarch of Constantinople. There his outspoken moralism made him a reproach to both clergy and court so that he was deposed in 404 and exiled to Cucusus, near Antioch. The people of Antioch flocked to hear their former spiritual guide, and he was exiled once again in 407, this time to a remote spot on the Black Sea. He died en route from the rigors of the journey. John was perhaps the most eloquent preacher of Christian antiquity; his sobriquet Chrysostom means the "golden-mouthed."

FROM *Exposition of Psalm 41*

When God saw that most men were slothful, that they came unwillingly to spiritual readings, and that they found the effort involved to be distasteful, wishing to make the labor more grateful and to allay its tedium he blended melody with prophecy in order that, delighted by the modulation of the chant, all might raise sacred hymns to him with great eagerness. For nothing so uplifts the mind, giving it wings and freeing it from the earth, releasing it from the prison of the body, affecting it with love of wisdom, and causing it to scorn all things pertaining to this life, as modulated melody and the divine chant composed of number.[1]

TEXT: Jacques Migne, ed., *Patrologia cursus completus. Series graeca*, vol. 55, cols. 155–59. Translation by Oliver Strunk, revised by James McKinnon.

1. In citing "modulated" melody, that is, properly measured melody, and chant composed of "number," John evokes typical ideas of classical Greek music theory, a subject that is characterized by a thoroughly mathematical conception of music.

To such an extent, indeed, is our nature delighted by chants and songs that even infants at the breast, if they be weeping or afflicted, are by reason of it lulled to slumber. Nurses, carrying them in their arms, walking to and fro and singing certain childish songs to them, cause their eyelids to close in sleep. For this reason travelers also sing as they drive their yoked animals at midday, thus lightening the hardships of the journey by their chants. And not only travelers, but peasants are accustomed to sing as they tread the grapes in the winepress, gather the vintage, tend the vine, and perform their other tasks. Sailors do likewise, pulling at the oars. Women, too, weaving and parting the tangled threads with the shuttle, often sing a particular melody, sometimes individually and to themselves, sometimes all together in concert. This they do—the women, travelers, peasants, and sailors—striving to lighten with a chant the labor endured in working, for the mind suffers hardships and difficulties more easily when it hears songs and chants.

Inasmuch as this kind of pleasure is thoroughly innate to our mind, and lest demons introducing lascivious songs should overthrow everything, God established the Psalms, in order that they might provide both pleasure and profit. From strange chants come harm, ruin, and many a dreadful thing, since what is lascivious and vicious in these songs settles in the recesses of the soul, making it softer and weaker; from the spiritual Psalms, however, proceeds much of value, much utility, much sanctity, and every inducement to philosophy, for the words purify the soul and the Holy Spirit descends swiftly upon the soul of the singer. For those who sing with understanding invoke the grace of the Spirit.

Hear what Paul says: "Be not drunk with wine, wherein is excess, but be filled with the Spirit." He adds, moreover, what the cause of this filling is: "Singing and making melody in your heart to the Lord."[2] What is the meaning of "in your heart"? With understanding, he says; not so that the mouth utters words while the mind is inattentive and wanders in all directions, but so that the mind may hear the tongue.

And as swine flock together where there is mud, and bees linger where there is aroma and incense, so demons congregate where there are licentious chants; but where there are spiritual ones there the grace of the Spirit descends, sanctifying mouth and soul. This I say, not only that you may yourselves sing praises, but also that you may teach your wives and children to do so, not merely to lighten the work while weaving, but especially at the table. For since Satan is wont to lie in wait at feasts, and to employ as allies drunkenness, gluttony, immoderate laughter, and an inactive mind; on these occasions, both before and after table, it is especially necessary to fortify oneself with the protection of the psalms and, rising from the feast together with one's wife and children, to sing sacred hymns to God.

2. Ephesians 5:18–19.

For if Paul—imprisoned, made fast in the stocks, and threatened with intolerable scourges—praised God along with Silas continually throughout the night (when sleep is most pleasant to everyone); and if neither the place, nor the hour, nor his anxieties, nor the tyrant's slumbers, nor the pain of his labors, nor anything else could bring him to interrupt his singing,[3] so much the more ought we, who live pleasantly and enjoy God's blessings, to give forth hymns that express thanks to him.

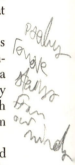

If something untoward be visited upon our souls because of drunkenness and gluttony, the arrival of psalmody will cause these evil and depraved counsels to retreat. And just as many wealthy persons wipe off their tables with a sponge filled with balsam, so that if any stain remain from the food, they may remove it and show a clean table; so should we also, filling our mouths with spiritual melody instead of balsam, so that if any stain remain in our mind from the abundance we may thereby wipe it away.

And let us all stand together and say: "For thou, Lord, hast made me glad by thy work; I will rejoice in the works of thy hands."[4] Then after the psalmody let there be added a prayer, in order that along with the soul we may also make holy the house itself.

And as those who bring comedians, dancers, and harlots into their feasts call in demons and Satan himself and fill their homes with innumerable contentions (among them jealousy, adultery, debauchery, and countless evils); so those who invoke David with his lyre call inwardly on Christ. Where Christ is, no demon would dare to enter, nor even to peep in; but peace, and charity, and all good things would flow there as from fountains. Those make their home a theater; you make yours a church. For where there are psalms, and prayers, and the dance of the prophets, and singers with pious intentions, no one will err if he calls such an assembly a church.

Even though the meaning of the words be unknown to you, teach your mouth to utter them; for the tongue is made holy by the words when they are spoken with a ready and eager mind. Once we have acquired this habit, we will not neglect so beautiful an office either deliberately or through carelessness; custom will compel us, even against our will, to carry out this worship daily. Nor will anyone, in such singing, be blamed if he be feeble from old age or too young, or have a harsh voice, or be totally lacking in the knowledge of rhythm.[5] What is sought for here is a sober spirit, an alert mind, a contrite heart, sound reason, and clear conscience; if having these you have entered into God's sacred choir, you may stand beside David himself.

Here there is no need for the cithara, or for stretched strings, or for the plectrum and technique, or for any musical instrument; but, if you like, you

3. Acts 16:25.
4. Psalm 91(92):4.
5. See note 1 above; rhythm is probably meant here more as the knowledge of durational proportions than the sensation of musical pulse.

become a cithara ~~...~~

*don't need ~~header~~
purpose more imp ?*

may yourself become a cithara by mortifying the members of the flesh and making a full harmony of mind and body.[6] For when the flesh no longer lusts against the spirit,[7] but has submitted to its orders and has been led at length into the best and most admirable path, then will you create a spiritual melody.

Here there is no need for technique which is slowly perfected; there is need only for lofty purpose, and we shall become skilled in a brief decisive moment. Here there is no need for place or for season; in all places and at all seasons you may sing with the mind. For whether you walk in the marketplace, or begin a journey, or sit down with your friends you may rouse up your spirit or call out silently. So also Moses called out, and God heard him.[8] If you are an artisan, you may sing while sitting and working in your shop. If you are a soldier, or if you sit in judgment, you may do the very same. One may also sing without voice, as the mind resounds inwardly. For we sing, not to men, but to God, who can hear our hearts and enter into the silences of our minds.

In proof of this, Paul cries out: "Likewise the Spirit helps us in our infirmities. And he who searches the hearts of men knows what is the mind of the Spirit, because the Spirit intercedes for the saints according to the will of God."[9] This does not mean that the Spirit groans; it means that spiritual men— having the gifts of the Spirit, praying for their kinsmen, and offering supplications—do so with contrition and groanings. Let us also do this, daily conversing with God in psalms and prayers. And let us not offer mere words, but let us know the very meaning of our discourse.

6. Another instance of instrumental allegory; see p. 12, note 3.
7. Galatians 5:17.
8. Exodus 14:15.
9. Romans 8:26–27.

3 St. Jerome

Eusebius Sophronius Hieronymus, now known as St. Jerome, was born of wealthy Christian parents about 340 C.E. at Stridon in Dalmatia. He spent his teenage years in Rome studying Greek philosophy and Latin literature under the famed grammarian Donatus. Attracted to the ascetical life, he sojourned in Trier and Aquileia for a number of years in quasi-monastic communities. In about 374 he set out to visit Jerusalem, but was detained by illness at Antioch. During the next several years, living in Antioch, the nearby deserts, and in Constantinople, he perfected his Greek, became more deeply involved in the practice of asceticism, and began the study of Hebrew. From 382 to 385 he lived in Rome where he became the confidant and secretary of Pope Damasus, who commissioned him to revise the Latin texts of the Bible. In 386 Jerome settled in Bethlehem where he founded a monastery over which he presided as he continued his work of biblical translation and commentary until his death in 420.

Jerome, an irascible personality, was an aggressive theological polemicist and a rigorous spiritual advisor, but he is best remembered as a biblical scholar. He was unique among the Christians of his time in his command of Hebrew and his interest in biblical history and archeology. His translation of the Bible, the Vulgate, has endured into modern times as the standard Latin version.

FROM *Commentary on the Epistle of Paul to the Ephesians*

"Speaking to yourselves in psalms and hymns and spiritual canticles, singing and making melody in your heart to the Lord."[1] He who has kept himself from the drunkenness of wine, wherein is excess, and has thereby been filled with the Spirit, is able to accept all things spiritually—psalms, hymns, and canticles.[2] How the psalm, the hymn, and the song differ from one another we learn most fully in the Psalter. Here let us say briefly that hymns declare the power and majesty of the Lord and continually praise his works and favors, something that is done by all those psalms to which the word *Alleluia* is prefixed or appended. Psalms, moreover, properly affect the ethical seat, so that by this organ of the body we may know what ought to be done and what avoided. But he who treats of higher things, the subtle investigator who explains the harmony of the world and the order and concord of all creatures, this one sings a spiritual song. For surely, to speak more plainly than we might wish for the sake of the simple, the psalm is directed to the body and the canticle to the mind. We ought, then, to sing and to make melody and to praise the Lord more with the spirit than with the voice.

This, indeed, is what is written: "Singing and making melody in your heart to the Lord." Let youth hear this, let them hear it whose office it is to sing in the church: sing to God, not with the voice, but with the heart; not, after the fashion of tragedians, in smearing the throat with a sweet ointment, so that theatrical melodies and songs are heard in the church, but in fear, in work, and in knowledge of the Scriptures. And although a man be *kakophonos*, to use a common expression, if he have good works, he is a sweet singer before God. And let the servant of Christ sing so that he pleases, not through his voice, but

TEXT: Jacques Migne, ed., *Patrologia cursus completus. Series latina*, vol. 26, cols. 561–62. Translation by Oliver Strunk, revised by James McKinnon.

1. 2 Ephesians 5:19. See also Colossians 3:16.
2. Psalms, hymns, and canticles are not to be understood in the modern sense of psalms from the Psalter, newly-composed hymns, and biblical canticles; they are rather different categories of psalms, that are suggested by superscriptions in the Psalter. For other passages where patristic writers develop the same sort of distinctions, see James McKinnon, *Music in Early Christian Literature* (Cambridge: Cambridge University Press, 1987), items 272, 359, and 360.

through the words which he pronounces, in order that the evil spirit which was in Saul[3] may be cast out from those who are similarly possessed by it, and may not enter into those who would make of the house of God a popular theater.

3. 1 Samuel 16:23.

4 Niceta of Remesiana

Niceta was born in the Roman province of Dacia during the second quarter of the fourth century C.E. He was named bishop of Remesiana (present-day Bela Palanka in Serbia) about 370 and died there after 414. Although a churchman and theologian of some standing in his own time, his works came to be misattributed, with the result that he was forgotten until the twentieth century. His sermon on psalmody quoted here, for example, appears as the third item in Martin Gerbert's *Scriptores ecclesiastici de musica* (1784), but in a badly defective version attributed to the sixth-century Nicetius of Trèves. The sermon is one of a pair. In the first of the two, "Concerning Vigils," Niceta had promised to devote an entire sermon on the psalm-singing practiced at these ceremonies; he kept his promise with "On the Benefit of Psalmody," a remarkable summary of the early Christian doctrine on ecclesiastical song.

FROM *On the Benefit of Psalmody*

I know of some, not only in our region but in the East, who consider the singing of psalms and hymns to be an excess that is barely appropriate to divine religion; they consider it enough if a psalm is spoken in the heart, and frivolous if uttered aloud by the mouth. They appropriate to their view that passage which the Apostle wrote to the Ephesians: "Be filled with the Spirit, speaking in psalms, hymns, and spiritual canticles, singing and making melody to the Lord in your hearts."[1] Look, they say, the apostle makes it clear that a psalm is to be sung in the heart, not prattled like the tunes of an actor, because it is enough for God "who searches the heart"[2] if it is sung there in secret. Nevertheless, if truth be told, just as I do not censure those who "sing in the heart" (for it is always beneficial to meditate upon the things of God), so too do I commend those who honor God with the sound of the voice.

TEXT: Cuthbert Turner, "Niceta of Remesiana II. Introduction and text of *De psalmodiae bono*," *Journal of Theological Studies* 24 (1922–1923): 233–41. Translation by James McKinnon.

1. Ephesians 5:18–19.
2. Romans 8:27.

Before I provide the testimony of numerous passages from Scripture, I shall, by reversing the interpretation of that very passage of the apostle that many use against singers, refute their foolishness. The Apostle says in fact: "Be filled with the Spirit as you speak," and I contend that the Spirit has freed our mouths, loosened our tongues, and opened our lips, for it is not possible for men to speak without these organs; and as heat differs from cold, so does silence from speaking. When, moreover, he adds, "speaking in psalms, hymns, and canticles," he would not have mentioned "canticles" *(canticorum)* if he had intended the singing to be altogether silent, because no one can sing *(cantare)* without making a sound. And when he says "in your hearts," he enjoins you not to sing only with the voice and without the heart, but as he says in another place, "I will sing with the Spirit, I will sing with understanding,"[3] that is, with both voice and thought.

•　　•　　•　　•　　•

If we enquire as to who first introduced this sort of song, we would find none other than Moses, who sang a splendid canticle to God after Egypt had been struck by the ten plagues, Pharoah had been drowned, and the people had been led along a miraculous pathway through the sea and into the desert; filled with gratitude he proclaimed, "Let us sing to the Lord, for he has triumphed gloriously."[4] For one ought not rashly to accept the volume called "The Inquiry of Abraham," where Abraham, along with animals, fountains, and the elements, is portrayed singing,[5] because this book is supported by neither faith nor any other authority. Moses, therefore, the leader of the tribes of Israel, was the first to establish choruses; he taught both sexes in separate groups to sing a triumphal canticle to God, while he and his sister went before them.[6] Afterwards one finds Deborah, an estimable woman, performing this ministry in the Book of Judges.[7] Again, Moses himself, as he was about to depart from his body, sang a fearsome song in the Book of Deuteronomy;[8] he left it to the people as a written testament, whereby the tribes of Israel would know what manner of deaths threatened them should they depart from the Lord . . .

After this you will find many, not only men but women as well, who were filled with the divine Spirit of God and sang of mysteries, this even before David, who, singled out by the Lord for this service from childhood, was found worthy to be a leader of singers and a treasury of song. While still a youth he played sweetly yet strongly upon the cithara and subdued the evil spirit that worked within Saul[9]—not because the cithara possessed such power, but

3. 1 Corinthians 14:15.
4. Exodus 15:1.
5. See the apocryphal Apocalypse of Abraham 17:6–18:14.
6. Miriam the prophetess, sister of Moses and Aaron, took a timbrel in hand and led the women in a canticle after the completion of Moses's canticle; see Exodus 15:20–21.
7. Judges 5:1–31.
8. Deuteronomy 32:1–43.
9. 1 Samuel 16:23.

because the image of Christ's cross was mystically exhibited in the wood and stretched strings of the instrument, and thereby it was the very Passion that was hymned and that overcame the spirit of the demon.

•   •   •   •   •

It would be tedious, dearly beloved, were I to recount every episode from the history of the Psalms, especially since it is necessary now to offer something from the New Testament in confirmation of the Old, lest one think the ministry of psalmody to be forbidden, inasmuch as many of the usages of the Old Law have been abolished. For those things that are carnal have been rejected, circumcision for example, and the observance of the Sabbath, sacrifices, discrimination among foods, as well as trumpets, citharas, cymbals, and tympana (all of which are now understood to reside in the bodily members of man, and there better to sound).[10] Daily ablutions, observance of new moons, the meticulous examination of leprosy, or whatever of this sort was necessary at the time for children,[11] have clearly ceased and gone their way. But the remaining practices that are spiritual, such as faith, piety, prayer, fasting, patience, chastity, and praise in song; these have been increased rather than diminished.

Hence you will find in the Gospels first Zacharias, father of the mighty John, to have voiced a prophetic hymn after his long silence.[12] Nor did Elizabeth, who had long been barren, cease to "magnify" God from her "soul" after her promised son had been born.[13] When Christ was born on earth a host of angels sang in praise of him, saying, "Glory to God in the highest," and proclaiming, "peace on earth to men of good will."[14] "The boys in the Temple cried out 'Hosanna to the son of David,'" nor did the Lord give in to the indignation of the loudly objecting Pharisees, and close the mouths of these innocents, but rather he opened them, saying, "Have you not read what was written, that 'Out of the mouth of babes and sucklings you have brought forth perfect praise,'"[15] and "'if these were silent the very stones would cry out.'"[16] Finally, not to prolong this discourse, the Lord himself, a teacher in words and a master in deeds, in order to display his approval of the sweet ministry of hymns, "went out to the Mount of Olives with his disciples after singing a hymn."[17]

10. Still another example of instrumental allegorical exegesis; see note 3 above in the passage from St. Basil, p. 12.

11. The reference to the religious observances of the Hebrew Scriptures as necessary to hold the attention of spiritual children was a commonplace—not without its anti-Semitic dimension—of fourth-century historical exegesis; for a more explicit example, see McKinnon, *Music in Early Christian Literature*, items 229–231.

12. Luke 1:67–79.

13. Luke 1:46. A confusing reference; it was Mary, not her cousin Elizabeth, who sang "My soul magnifies the Lord" on the occasion of her visit to Elizabeth, and Elizabeth's son John was not yet born at the time.

14. Luke 2:13–14.

15. Matthew 21:15–16.

16. Luke 19:40.

17. Matthew 26:30 and Mark 14:26.

. . . . .

What could be more appropriate than this kind of benefit? For we are pleasured by psalms, bedewed by prayers, and fed by the interspersed readings. Indeed, just as the honest guests at a banquet are delighted with a succession of courses, so are our souls nourished by a variety of readings and a display of hymns.

Then let us, dearly beloved, sing psalms with alert senses and awakened minds, as the hymnodist exhorts us: "Since God is King over all the earth, sing psalms with understanding,"[18] for a psalm is sung not only "in spirit," that is, with the sound of the voice, but also "in mind,"[19] so that we think of what we sing, rather than allow the mind, caught up in distractions (as often happens), to lose the fruit of its labor. Let the chant, then, be sung in a manner befitting holy religion; let it not display theatrical turgidity, but show a Christian simplicity in its melody, and let it not evoke the stage, but create compunction in the listeners. Our voices ought not to be dissonant, but concordant—not with one dragging out the song, and another cutting it short, while one sings too softly, and another too loudly—and all must seek to blend their voices within the sound of a harmonious chorus, not to project it outward in vulgar display like a cithara. It must all be done as if in the sight of God, not man, and not to please oneself.

We have a model and exemplar of this vocal consonance in those three blessed youths of whom the Book of Daniel speaks: "Then these three as if from one voice sang a hymn and glorified God in the furnace saying, 'Blessed art thou, the God of our Fathers.' "[20] You have it here on biblical authority that the three praised the Lord together "as if from one voice," just as all of us must exhibit the same intention and the same sounding melody as if from a single voice. Those, however, who are not able to blend and adapt themselves to the others, ought better to sing in a subdued voice than to create a great clamor; and thus will they fulfill their liturgical obligation and avoid disrupting the singing community. For it is not given to all to possess a supple and pleasant voice.

18. Psalm 46(47):8.
19. "I will sing with the spirit, and I will sing with the mind"; 1 Corinthians 15:15.
20. Daniel 3:51–52; the long passage that has the canticle of the three youths is present only in the Greek-Latin-Catholic textual tradition, not in the Hebrew-Protestant tradition.

5 St. Augustine

Aurelius Augustinus was born at Tagaste in North Africa in 354 C.E. to a pagan father and Christian mother, the sainted Monica. In 384, after several years of spiritual crisis and philosophical enquiry during which he lost his childhood faith and maintained a relationship with the mistress who bore his son Adeodatus, he settled in Milan as a professor of rhetoric. There he fell under the influence of St. Ambrose and was baptized in 387. Soon after, he returned to Africa where, following a period of monastic seclusion, he was ordained priest in 391 and four years later was consecrated bishop of Hippo Regius, present-day Annaba in Algeria. He died there in 430 while the city was under seige by the Vandals.

Augustine may be the most important figure in the history of Christian thought, seriously rivaled only by Thomas Aquinas. And while he is the author of numerous exegetical and theological works, and more than 800 preserved sermons, his intellectual influence is felt outside of the narrowly religious sphere as well: his *De musica* moves beyond classical metrics to a philosophy of rhythm; his *City of God* is a profound reflection on the nature of history; and his *Confessions* is an autobiography marked by a quality of psychological probing unknown before modern times. The passage from this last work that appears below shows the saint torn between feelings of guilt at the pleasure he experiences in hearing music and the position that sacred song is ultimately a beneficial practice.

FROM THE *Confessions*

The delights of the ear had enticed me and held me in their grip, but you have unbound and liberated me. Yet, I confess, I still surrender to some slight pleasure in those sounds to which your words give life, when they are sung by a sweet and skilled voice, but not so much that I cleave to them, unable to rise above them when I wish. But yet, these chants, animated as they are by your words, must gain entry to me and find in my heart a place of some dignity, even if I scarcely provide them a fitting one. Sometimes it seems to me that I grant them more honor than is proper, when I sense that the words stir my soul to greater religious fervor and to a more ardent piety if they are thus sung than if not thus sung, and when I feel that all the diverse affections of my soul have their own proper measures in voice and song, which are stimulated by I

TEXT: Lucas Verheijen, ed., *Sancti Augustini Confessiones Libri XIII*, Corpus Christianorum Series Latina 27 (Turnhout: Brepols, 1981), pp. 181–82. Translation of this selection (Book 10, Chapter 33) by James McKinnon.

know not what hidden correspondences.[1] But the gratification of the flesh—to which I ought not surrender my mind to be enervated—frequently leads me astray, for the senses are not content to accompany reason by patiently following it, but after being admitted only for the sake of reason, they seek to rush ahead and lead it. I sin thus in these things unknowingly, but afterwards I do know.

Sometimes, however, overly anxious to avoid this particular snare, I err by excessive severity, and sometimes so much so that I wish every melody of those sweet chants to which the songs of David are set, to be banished from my ears and from the very church. And it seems safer to me what I remember was often told me concerning Bishop Athanasius of Alexandria, who required the reader of the psalm to perform it with so little inflection of voice that it resembled speaking more than singing.[2]

Yet when I recall the tears that I shed at the song of the Church in the first days of my recovered faith, and even now as I am moved not by the song but by the things which are sung—when chanted with fluent voice and completely appropriate melody—I acknowledge the great benefit of this practice. Thus I waver between the peril of pleasure and the benefit of my experience; but I am inclined, while not maintaining an irrevocable position, to endorse the custom of singing in church so that weaker souls might rise to a state of devotion by indulging their ears. Yet when it happens that I am moved more by the song than by what is sung, I confess to sinning grievously, and I would prefer not to hear the singer at such times. See now my condition! Weep with me and weep for me, you who cultivate within yourselves the good will whence good deeds proceed (for if you are not so disposed, my words will fail to move you). But you, my Lord and my God, give ear, look and see, have pity on me and heal me, you before whom I have become an enigma unto my self—and that is my very infirmity.

1. There is an echo of Platonic musical psychology in this latter clause that speaks of a causal relationship, almost physical and mechanical, between certain thoughts and feelings and certain musical melodies and rhythms. The belief in this sort of relationship is generally referred to as "ethos doctrine." See, for example, Plato's *Republic* 398–403 (*SR*1).
2. St. Athanasius was bishop of Alexandria intermittently from 328 to his death in 373; for examples of his somewhat severe ideas on psalmody see McKinnon, *Music in Early Christian Literature,* items 98–100.

MUSIC AS A LIBERAL ART

6 Boethius

Anicius Manlius Severinus Boethius was born to a noble Roman family in about 480. Through a combination of his own birthright, his marriage into the powerful Symmachus family, and his extraordinary talents, he rose quickly in the political hierarchy of the time. He held the consulship in 510 and eventually became a friend and advisor of the Gothic king Theodoric. He fell under suspicion, however, of cooperating with Byzantine designs upon Gothic Italy; he was imprisoned at Pavia in 523 and executed sometime between 524 and 526.

Boethius is the primary figure in the transition between the intellectual worlds of Classical Antiquity and the Middle Ages. His works include treatises on the four mathematical arts of the quadrivium, on logic, and on various theological subjects, as well as his immensely popular *On the Consolation of Philosophy,* written during his imprisonment. His *Fundamentals of Music,* largely a translation and paraphrase of Nichomachus and Ptolemy, is one of the four quadrivial treatises; it had a far-reaching influence upon the development of medieval musical theory. Translated here are excerpts from the less technical portions of the work. (The entire treatise is translated by Calvin M. Bower, *Fundamentals of Music: Anicius Manlius Severinus Boethius* [New Haven: Yale University Press, 1989].)

FROM *Fundamentals of Music*

BOOK ONE

1. INTRODUCTION: MUSIC IS RELATED TO US BY NATURE AND CAN ENNOBLE OR CORRUPT THE CHARACTER

The perceptive power of all the senses is so spontaneously and naturally present in certain living creatures that to conceive of an animal without senses is impossible. Yet an inquiry by the mind will not provide to the same degree a knowledge and clear understanding of the senses themselves. It is easily understood that we use our senses to perceive sensible things, but the very nature of the senses by which we act, as well as the peculiar property of sensible things, is not so apparent or intelligible save by proper investigation and reflection upon the truth.

Sight is common to all mortals, but whether it results from images coming to the eye or from rays sent out to the object of sight is doubtful to the learned, though the vulgar are unaware that such doubt exists. Again, anyone seeing a triangle or square easily recognizes what he sees, but to know the nature of a square or triangle he must inquire of a mathematician.

TEXT: Gottfried Friedlein, ed., *Anicii Manliii Torquate Severini Boetii De Institutione Arithmetica Libri Duo De Institutione Musica Libri Quinque* (Leipzig, 1867), pp. 178–89, 223–25. Translation by William Strunk, Jr., and Oliver Strunk, revised by James McKinnon.

The same may be said of other matters of sense, especially of the judgment of the ear, whose power so apprehends sounds that it not only judges them and knows their differences, but is often delighted when the modes[1] are sweet and well-ordered, and pained when disordered and incoherent ones offend the sense.

From this it follows that, of the four mathematical disciplines, the others are concerned with the pursuit of truth, but music is related not only to speculation but to morality as well. Nothing is more characteristic of human nature than to be soothed by sweet modes and disturbed by their opposites. Nor is this limited to particular professions or ages; it is, rather, common to all professions, while infants, youth, and the old as well are so naturally attuned to musical modes by a kind of spontaneous feeling that no age is without delight in sweet song. From this may be discerned the truth of what Plato said, not idly, that the soul of the universe is united by musical concord.[2] For when we apprehend by means of what is well and fitly ordered in ourselves, that which is well and fitly combined in sounds—and take pleasure in this—we recognize that we ourselves are internally united by this congruity. For congruity is agreeable, incongruity hateful and contrary.

From this source, also, the greatest alterations of character arise. A lascivious mind takes pleasure in the more lascivious modes, and is often softened and corrupted by listening to them. Contrariwise, a sterner mind finds joy in the more stirring modes and is braced by them. This is why the musical modes are named after certain peoples, such as the Lydian and Phrygian; the mode takes the name of the nation that delights in it. For a people takes pleasure in modes resembling its own character, nor can it be that the soft should be joined to and delight the hard, or the hard delight the soft, but, as I have said, it is congruity which causes love and delight. For this reason Plato insists that any change in music of right moral tendency should be avoided, declaring that there could be no greater detriment to the morals of a community than a gradual perversion of modest and temperate music.[3] For the minds of the listeners are immediately affected and gradually go astray, retaining no trace of honesty and right, if either the lascivious modes implant in them something shameful or the harsher modes something savage and monstrous.

Discipline has no more open pathway to the mind than through the ear; when rhythms and modes gain access to the mind by this path, it is evident that they affect it and cause it to conform to their nature. One observes this among the nations. Ruder peoples delight in the harsher modes of the Thra-

---

1. Mode is a word with a wide variety of meanings in antiquity, although all of them, in keeping with the mathematical view of music predominating at the time, partake at least to some extent of the word's root meaning "measure." Here the word might convey something of the connotation of the Platonic *harmoniae* such as the Dorian and Phrygian, or it might simply refer to musical melody in a more general sense.
2. *Timaeus* 37A.
3. *Republic* 424B–424C.

cians, civilized peoples in more restrained modes; though in these days this almost never occurs. Since humanity is now soft and fickle, it is wholly captivated by the modes of the theater. Music was chaste and modest so long as it was played on simpler instruments, but since it has come to be performed in a protracted and confusing mixture of styles,[4] it has lost its grave and virtuous manner, descending virtually to depravity, and preserving only a trace of its ancient beauty.

This is why Plato prescribes that boys should not be trained in all modes, but only in those which are strong and simple.[5] And above all we should bear in mind that if something is altered even in the very slightest, it will—although not sensed at first—eventually make a considerable difference and will pass through the sense of hearing into the mind. Hence Plato holds that music which is carefully and modestly composed, so that it is chaste, simple, and masculine, not effeminate, savage, and inconsistent, is a great guardian of the commonwealth.[6]

· · · · ·

It is well known indeed how often song has overcome anger, and how many wonders it has performed on the affections of the body and mind. Who is unaware that Pythagoras, by means of a spondaic melody, calmed and restored to self-control a youth of Taormina who had become intoxicated by the sound of the Phrygian mode? One night a harlot was shut up in the house of the youth's rival, and he in his frenzy was about to set fire to it. Pythagoras, observing the motion of the stars as was his custom, learned that the youth, agitated by the sound of the Phrygian mode, was deaf to the many pleas of his friends to desist from his crime; he ordered that the mode be changed, and thus reduced the youth's fury to a state of perfect calm.

Cicero, in his *De consiliis*, tells the story differently, in this manner: "But if I may, struck by some similarity, compare a trifling matter to a weighty one, it is said that when certain drunken youths, aroused, as is wont to happen, by the music of the tibia,[7] were about to break into the house of a modest woman, Pythagoras urged the player to perform a spondaic melody. When he had done this, the slowness of the measures and the gravity of the player calmed their wanton fury."[8]

To add a few brief illustrations in the same vein, Terpander and Arion of Methymna rescued the Lesbians and the Ionians from the gravest maladies by the aid of song. Then Ismenias the Theban, when the torments of sciatica

---

4. The Latin *tractatam varie et permixte* is cryptic; it seems to suggest the mixing of the musical genres, something that Plato considered to be the most serious of musical perversions; see the *Laws* 700a–701b.
5. *Republic* 399C. See *SR1*.
6. *Republic* 401D. See *SR1*.
7. The tibia is the Latin equivalent of the Greek aulos, the most common wind instrument of antiquity; it is frequently mistranslated flute although it was a reed instrument.
8. The passage does not appear to be from Cicero's *De consiliis*.

were troubling a number of Boeotians, is reported to have rid them of all their afflictions by his melodies. And Empedocles, when an infuriated youth drew his sword upon a guest of his who had passed sentence upon his father, is said to have altered the mode of the singing and thus to have tempered the young man's anger.

Indeed, the power of the musical art became so evident through the studies of ancient philosophy that the Pythagoreans used to free themselves from the cares of the day by certain melodies, which caused a gentle and quiet slumber to steal upon them. Similarly, upon rising, they dispelled the stupor and confusion of sleep by certain other melodies, knowing that the whole structure of soul and body is united by musical harmony.

·   ·   ·   ·   ·

Is it not evident that the spirit of warriors is roused by the sound of the trumpets? If it is true that a peaceful state of mind can be converted into wrath and fury, then beyond doubt a gentler mode can temper the anger and passionate desire of a perturbed mind. How does it happen that when someone willingly takes in a song with both the ears and the spirit, he is involuntarily turned to it, so that his body feigns some motion similar to that of the song heard, and how does it happen that his spirit picks out simply with its memory some previously heard melody. From all this it appears clear and certain that music is so much a part of our nature that we cannot do without it even if we wish to do so.

The power of the mind should therefore be directed to the purpose of comprehending by science what is inherent by nature. Just as in seeing, the learned are not content to behold colors and forms without investigating their properties, so they are not content to be delighted by melodies without learning what pitch ratios render them internally consistent.

2. THE THREE KINDS OF MUSIC, WITH A CONSIDERATION OF THE POWER OF MUSIC

A writer on music should therefore state at the beginning how many kinds of music those who have investigated the subject are known to have recognized. There are three kinds: the first, the music of the universe; the second, human music; the third, instrumental music, as that of the cithara or the tibia or the other instruments which serve for melody.

The first, the music of the universe, is especially to be studied in the combining of the elements and the variety of the seasons which are observed in the heavens. How indeed could the swift mechanism of the sky move silently in its course? And although this sound does not reach our ears (as must for many reasons be the case), the extremely rapid motion of such great bodies could not be altogether silent, especially since the courses of the stars are joined together by such mutual adaptation that nothing more equally compacted or united could be imagined. For some orbit higher and others lower, and all revolve by a common impulse, so that an established order of their circuits can be deduced from their various inequalities. For this reason an established order of modulation[9] cannot be lacking in this celestial revolution.

Now unless a certain harmony united the differences and contrary powers of the four elements, how could they form a single body and mechanism? But all this diversity produces the variety of seasons and fruits, yet thereby makes the year a unity. So if you could imagine any one of the elements that produce such a variety removed, all would perish, nor, so to speak, would they retain a vestige of consonance. And just as there is a careful adjustment of pitch in low strings lest the lowness descend to inaudibility, and an adjustment of tension in high strings lest, being too taut, they be broken by the rarified pitch, (while all remains congruous and fitting); similarly we perceive that in the music of the universe nothing can be so extreme as to destroy some other part by its own excess, but each part brings its own contribution or aids others to bring theirs. For what winter binds, spring releases, and what summer heats, autumn ripens; the seasons in turn bring forth their own fruits or help others to bring forth theirs. These matters will be discussed more searchingly later on.

What human music is, anyone may understand by examining his own nature. For what is that which unites the incorporeal activity of the reason with the body, unless it be a certain mutual adaptation and as it were a tempering of low and high sounds into a single consonance? What else joins together the parts of the soul itself, which in the opinion of Aristotle is a union of the rational and the irrational?[10] What causes the blending of the body's elements or holds its parts together in established adaptation? This also I shall take up later.

The third kind of music is that which is described as residing in certain instruments. This is produced by tension, as in strings, or by blowing, as in the tibia or in those instruments activated by water,[11] or by some kind of percussion, as in instruments where one beats upon a bronze concavity;[12] by such means various sounds are produced.

It seems best in this work to treat first of the music of instruments.[13] But enough of introduction. The elements of music themselves must now be discussed.

• • • • •

9. "Modulation" is a translation of *modulatio*, literally, measuring; it appears here to have the meaning of music in general, although, again, with mathematical connotation. At other places in this volume, *modulatio*, as suggested by the context, is translated "measurement."
10. *On the Soul* 423A.
11. Boethius has in mind here the hydraulis, or water organ, an instrument that he may have known only from literary references.
12. An apparent reference to the *cymbala* of antiquity, a pair of small cup-shaped cymbals.
13. Boethius moves on, then, not to a study of instrumental music, but to a study of pitch (the discipline of harmonics, that is) as demonstrated on instruments.

33. WHAT A MUSICIAN IS

It should be borne in mind that every art, and every discipline as well, has by nature a more honorable character than a handicraft, which is produced by the hand and labor of a craftsman.[14] For it is far greater and nobler to know what someone does than to accomplish oneself what someone else knows, for physical skill obeys like a handmaid while reason rules like a mistress. And unless the hand does what the mind sanctions, it acts in vain. How much more admirable, then, is the science of music in apprehending by reason than in accomplishing by work and deed! It is as much nobler as the body is surpassed by the mind, because the person destitute of reason lives in servitude. But reason reigns and leads to what is right; and unless its rule is obeyed, a work thus deprived of reason will falter. It follows, then, that reason's contemplation of working does not need the deed, while the works of our hands are nothing unless guided by reason.

How great the glory and merit of reason are can be understood from this: that those so-called physical craftsmen take their names, not from their discipline, but rather from their instruments. For the citharodist is named after the cithara, the aulodist after the tibia,[15] and the others after the names of their instruments. He however is a musician who has absorbed the science of singing by careful reflection, not by the servitude of work but by the rule of contemplation. We see the same thing in the erection of buildings and the waging of wars, namely in the contrary conferring of names: the buildings are inscribed and the triumphs held in the names of those by whose rule and reason they were begun, not of those by whose labor and servitude they were completed.

Thus there are three classes concerned with the art of music. One class has to do with instruments, another invents songs, a third judges the work of instruments and the song. But that class which is dedicated to instruments and there consumes its entire efforts, as for example the players of the cithara and those who show their skill on the organ and other musical instruments, are cut off from the understanding of musical science, since they are servants, as has been said, who do not make any use of reason, and are altogether lacking in thought. The second class having to do with music is that of the poets, which is attracted to song not so much by speculation and reason as by a certain natural instinct. Thus this class also is to be separated from music. The third is that which acquires the skill of judging, so that it weighs rhythms and melodies and the whole of song. And this class is rightly reckoned as musical because it relies entirely upon reason and speculation. And that person is a musician who possesses the faculty of judging—according to speculation and reason that is

---

14. There is more than an echo here of the classical prejudice, one with a long life in the Western European tradition, that the "liberal arts" are those practiced by individuals who have the leisure to cultivate the things of the mind, free as they are from the necessity to use their hands in making a living; see Aristotle, *Politics* 1337b–1338a. See *SR1*.
15. See note 7 above.

appropriate and suitable to music—of modes and rhythms, of the classes of melodies and their combinations,[16] of all those things about which there is to be discussion later on, and of the songs of the poets.

16. *Permixtionibus* is rendered "combinations" here because it seems to fit the context well even though the mixing of musical genres is forbidden by Plato; see note 4 above. Calvin M. Bower makes a plausible case for consonance; see his *Fundamentals of Music*, p. 51.

7 Cassiodorus

Flavius Magnus Aurelius Cassiodorus was born to a noble Roman family in about 490 C.E. at Squillace on the Ionian Sea. He served, as did Boethius, in the Gothic court of Theodoric, but managed to outlive his patron, who died in 526, not long after the execution of Boethius. Cassiodorus spent the dangerous years of the Gothic Wars in Constantinople, returning to Italy in 554 to settle at his monastery at Vivarium, near his native Squillace, where he died in about 583.

Cassiodorus, like Boethius, is one of the principal figures in the transmission of ancient culture to the Latin Middle Ages. Of musical interest among his works are the *Exposition of the Psalms*, written during his eastern sojourn, and the *Fundamentals of Sacred and Secular Learning*, written at Vivarium. The latter, intended as a primer for the monks under his charge, is divided into two books. The first is more directly concerned with religious studies, while the second provides brief summaries of the seven liberal arts. The section on music, given below, is much more superficial than Boethius's work, but was nonetheless influential in the formation of medieval musical thought, particularly in its earlier stages.

FROM *Fundamentals of Sacred and Secular Learning*

V. OF MUSIC

1. A certain Gaudentius, writing on music, says that Pythagoras found its beginning in the sound of hammers and the striking of stretched strings.[1] Muti-

TEXT: R. A. B. Mynors, ed., *Institutiones divinarum et saecularium litterarum* (Oxford: Clarendon Press, 1937), pp. 142–50. Translation by William Strunk, Jr., and Oliver Strunk, revised by James McKinnon.

1. On the topos of the "inventors of music" see James W. McKinnon, *"Jubal vel Pythagoras, quis sit inventor musicae:* Thoughts on Musical Historiography from Boethius to Burney," *The Musical Quarterly* 64 (1978): 1–28.

anus, a man of great eloquence, has translated the work of Gaudentius into Latin in a manner attesting his skill. Clement the Alexandrian priest declares in his *Exhortation to the Greeks* that music received its origin from the Muses, and takes pains to make clear for what reason the Muses themselves were invented: they were so named ἀπὸ τοῦ μῶσθαι, that is, "from inquiring," because, as the ancients would have it, they were the first to inquire into the power of songs and the modulation of the voice.[2] We find also that Censorinus, in his treatise *De die natali,* addressed to Quintus Cerellius, has written things not to be overlooked concerning the musical discipline, or the second part of mathematics,[3] hence it is profitable to read him so that these things are more deeply implanted in the mind by frequent meditation.

2. The discipline of music is diffused through all the actions of our life. First, it is true that if we perform the commandments of the Creator and with pure minds obey the rules he has laid down, then every word we speak, every pulsation of our veins, is related by musical rhythms to the powers of harmony. Music indeed is the knowledge of proper measurement.[4] If we live virtuously, we are constantly proved to be under its discipline, but when we commit injustice we are without music. The heavens and the earth, indeed all things in them which are directed by a higher power, share in this discipline of music, for Pythagoras shows that this universe was founded by and can be governed by music.

3. Music is closely bound up with religion itself. Witness the decachord of the Ten Commandments,[5] the tinkling of cithara and tympanum, the melody of the organ, the sound of cymbals.[6] The very Psalter is without doubt named after a musical instrument because the exceedingly sweet and pleasing melody of the celestial virtues is contained within it.

4. Let us now discuss the parts of music, as it has been handed down from the elders. Musical science is the discipline which treats of numbers in their relation to those things which are found in sounds, such as duple, triple, quadruple, and others said to be similar to these.[7]

2. In point of fact, Clement reports that Alcman derived the origin of the Muses from Zeus and Mnemosyne; he does not speak of the origin of music (see his *Exhortation to the Greeks* 2). As for the etymology of ἀπὸ τοῦ μῶσθαι, this is from Plato, *Cratylus* 406A.

3. *De die natali* 13.1.

4. *Musica quippe est scientia bene modulandi.* The definition is from Augustine, *De musica* 1.2. There is no completely adequate translation for *bene modulari,* a phrase that is rich not only in aesthetic connotation but ethical and mathematical connotation as well.

5. Cassiodorus repeats a commonplace of patristic instrumental allegory: the psaltery of ten strings (Psalm 32:2) is taken to symbolize the Ten Commandments.

6. See Psalm 150:3–5.

7. *Musica scientia est disciplina quae de numeris loquitur qui ad aliquid sunt his qui inveniuntur in sonis, ut duplum, triplum, quadruplum, et his similia quae dicuntur ad aliquid.* This definition is designed to indicate the relation of music to the other divisions of mathematics and is an expansion of one that Cassiodorus had already given (2.3.21) in introducing the subject of the quadrivium. "Mathematical science . . . is that which considers abstract quantity. By abstract quantity we mean that quantity which we treat in a purely speculative way, separating it intellec-

5. The parts of music are three: harmonics, rhythmics, metrics. Harmonics is the musical science which distinguishes the high and low in sounds. Rhythmics is that which inquires whether words in combination sound well or badly together. Metrics is that which by valid reasoning knows the measures of the various meters; for example, the heroic, the iambic, the elegiac.

6. There are three classes of musical instruments: instruments of percussion, instruments of tension, and wind instruments. Instruments of percussion include cup-shaped vessels of bronze and silver, and others whose hard metal, when struck, yields an agreeable ringing. Instruments of tension are made with strings, held in place according to the rules of the art, which upon being struck by the plectrum delightfully soothe the ear. Among these are the various species of cithara. Wind instruments are those which are actuated to produce a vocal sound when filled by a stream of air, as trumpets, reeds, organs, pandoria,[8] and others of this nature.

7. We have still to explain the symphonies.[9] Symphony is the fusion of a low sound with a high one or of a high sound with a low one, an adaptation effected either vocally or by blowing or striking. There are six symphonies:

1) diatessaron	4) diapason and diatessaron together
2) diapente	5) diapason and diapente together
3) diapason	6) disdiapason

I. The consonance of the diatessaron results from the epitrita ratio (4:3) and includes four pitches, hence its name.

II. The consonance of the diapente results from the emiola ratio (3:2) and includes five pitches.

III. The consonance of the diapason, also called diocto, results from the displasia or dupla ratio (2:1) and includes eight pitches, hence the names diocto and diapason. And since the citharas of the ancients had eight strings, this consonance, including as it does all sounds, is called diapason (literally, through all).[10]

---

tually from its material and from its other accidents, such as evenness, oddness, and the like. It has these divisions: arithmetic, music, geometry, astronomy. Arithmetic is the discipline of absolute numerable quantity. Music is the discipline which treats of numbers in their relation to those things which are found in sounds. Geometry is the discipline of immobile magnitude and of forms. Astronomy is the discipline of the course of the heavenly bodies." Cassiodorus's definition of music clearly influences the terse one that is common in the Middle Ages: *Musica est de numero relato ad sonos* ("music has to do with number as related to sounds").

8. By *pandoria* Cassiodorus appears to have in mind the Latin term *pandura*, which refers to a type of lute; see James McKinnon, "Pandoura," *The New Grove Dictionary of Music and Musicians*, vol. 14, p. 154.

9. Symphony is a term with a long and varied history in Western music; here it appears in its simple root meaning as a "sounding with" or consonance.

10. But see the Pseudo-Aristotelian *Problems* 720A: "Why is the octave called the 'diapason' instead of being called the diocto according to the number of the notes, in the same way as the terms used for the fourth and fifth? Is it because originally there were seven strings? Then

IV. The consonance of the combined diapason and diatessaron results from the ratio which the number 24 has to the number 8[11] and includes eleven pitches.

V. The consonance of the combined diapason and diapente results from the triplasia ratio (3:1) and includes twelve pitches.

VI. The consonance of the disdiapason, that is double diapason, results from the tetraplasia ratio (4:1) and includes fifteen pitches.

8. Key is a difference or quantity of the whole harmonic system, consisting in the intonation or level of the voice.[12] There are fifteen keys:

Hypodorian	Dorian	Hyperdorian
Hypoiastian	Iastian	Hyperiastian
Hypophrygian	Phrygian	Hyperphrygian
Hypoaeolian	Aeolian	Hyperaeolian
Hypolydian	Lydian	Hyperlydian

I. The Hypodorian key is the one sounding lowest of all, for which reason it is also called lower.

II. The Hypoiastian exceeds the Hypodorian by a semitone.

III. The Hypophrygian exceeds the Hypoiastian by a semitone, the Hypodorian by a tone.

IV. The Hypoaeolian exceeds the Hypophrygian by a semitone, the Hypoiastian by a tone, the Hypodorian by a tone and a half.

V. The Hypolydian exceeds the Hypoaeolian by a semitone, the Hypophrygian by a tone, the Hypoiastian by a tone and a half, the Hypodorian by two tones.

VI. The Dorian exceeds the Hypolydian by a semitone, the Hypoaeolian by a tone, the Hypophrygian by a tone and a half, the Hypoiastian by two tones, the Hypodorian by two tones and a half, that is, by the consonance diatessaron.

VII. The Iastian exceeds the Dorian by a semitone, the Hypolydian by a tone, the Hypoaeolian by a tone and a half, the Hypophrygian by two tones, the Hypoiastian by two tones and a half, that is, by the consonance diatessaron, the Hypodorian by three tones.

VIII. The Phrygian exceeds the Iastian by a semitone, the Dorian by a tone, the Hypolydian by a tone and a half, the Hypoaeolian by two tones, the Hypophrygian by two tones and a half, that is, by the consonance diatessaron, the

---

Terpander took away the trite and added the nete, and at that time it was called the diapason, not the diocto, for there were seven notes." (Translation by W. S. Hett, *Aristotle: Problems* (London: Loeb Classical Library, 1961), vol. 1, p. 397.)

11. The correct ratio is 24:9 or 8:3.

12. "Key" *(tonus)* is a difficult subject in ancient music theory. Some theorists of Late Antiquity seem not to have understood it very well themselves, reducing it to nothing more than fifteen transpositions by a half-step of the entire tonal system. Here Cassiodorus provides the *reductio ad absurdum* of the subject in an exposition that will remind the modern reader of "The Twelve Days of Christmas."

Hypoiastian by three tones, the Hypodorian by three tones and a half, that is, by the consonance diapente.

IX. The Aeolian exceeds the Phrygian by a semitone, the Iastian by a tone, the Dorian by a tone and a half, the Hypolydian by two tones, the Hypoaeolian by two tones and a half, that is, by the consonance diatessaron, the Hypophrygian by three tones, the Hypoiastian by three tones and a half, that is, by the consonance diapente, the Hypodorian by four tones.

X. The Lydian exceeds the Aeolian by a semitone, the Phrygian by a tone, the Iastian by a tone and a half, the Dorian by two tones, the Hypolydian by two tones and a half, that is, by the consonance diatessaron, the Hypoaeolian by three tones, the Hypophrygian by three tones and a half, that is, by the consonance diapente, the Hypoiastian by four tones, the Hypodorian by four tones and a half.

XI. The Hyperdorian exceeds the Lydian by a semitone, the Aeolian by a tone, the Phrygian by a tone and a half, the Iastian by two tones, the Dorian by two tones and a half, that is, by the consonance diatessaron, the Hypolydian by three tones, the Hypoaeolian by three tones and a half, that is, by the consonance diapente, the Hypophrygian by four tones, the Hypoiastian by four tones and a half, the Hypodorian by five tones.

XII. The Hyperiastian exceeds the Hyperdorian by a semitone, the Lydian by a tone, the Aeolian by a tone and a half, the Phrygian by two tones, the Iastian by two tones and a half, that is, by the consonance diatessaron, the Dorian by three tones, the Hypolydian by three tones and a half, that is, by the consonance diapente, the Hypoaeolian by four tones, the Hypophrygian by four tones and a half, the Hypoiastian by five tones, the Hypodorian by five tones and a half.

XIII. The Hyperphrygian exceeds the Hyperiastian by a semitone, the Hyperdorian by a tone, the Lydian by a tone and a half, the Aeolian by two tones, the Phrygian by two tones and a half, that is, by the consonance diatessaron, the Iastian by three tones, the Dorian by three tones and a half, that is, by the consonance diapente, the Hypolydian by four tones, the Hypoaeolian by four tones and a half, the Hypophrygian by five tones, the Hypoiastian by five tones and a half, the Hypodorian by six tones, that is, by the consonance diapason.

XIV. The Hyperaeolian exceeds the Hyperphrygian by a semitone, the Hyperiastian by a tone, the Hyperdorian by a tone and a half, the Lydian by two tones, the Aeolian by two tones and a half, that is, by the consonance diatessaron, the Phrygian by three tones, the Iastian by three tones and a half, that is, by the consonance diapente, the Dorian by four tones, the Hypolydian by four tones and a half, the Hypoaeolian by five tones, the Hypophrygian by five tones and a half, the Hypoiastian by six tones, that is, by the consonance diapason, the Hypodorian by six tones and a half.

XV. The Hyperlydian, the newest and highest of all, exceeds the Hyperaeolian by a semitone, the Hyperphrygian by a tone, the Hyperiastian by a tone and a half, the Hyperdorian by two tones, the Lydian by two tones and a half, that is, by the consonance diatessaron, the Aeolian by three tones, the Phrygian by three tones and a half, that is, by the consonance diapente, the Iastian by four tones, the Dorian by four tones and a half, the Hypolydian by five tones, the Hypoaeolian by five tones and a half, the Hypophrygian by six tones, that is, by the consonance diapason, the Hypoiastian by six tones and a half, the Hypodorian by seven tones.

From this it appears that the Hyperlydian key, the highest of all, exceeds the Hypodorian, the lowest of all, by seven tones. So useful, Varro observes, is the power displayed by these keys that they can compose distraught minds and also attract the very beasts, serpents even, and birds, and dolphins, to listen to their melody.

9. But the lyre of Orpheus and the songs of the Sirens, we will pass over in silence as fables. Yet what shall we say of David, who freed Saul from the unclean spirit by the discipline of wholesome melody, and by a new method, through the sense of hearing, restored the king to the health which the physicians had been unable to bestow by the virtues of herbs? Asclepiades the physician, according to the ancients a most learned man, is remembered for having restored a man from frenzy to his former sanity by means of melody. We read of many other miracles that have been wrought upon the sick by this discipline. It is said that the heavens themselves, as we have recalled above, are made to revolve by sweet harmony. And to summarize all in a few words, nothing in things celestial or terrestrial which is fittingly conducted according to the Creator's own plan is found to be exempt from this discipline.

10. This study, therefore, which both lifts up our senses to celestial things and pleases our ears with sweet melody, is most gratifying and useful. Among the Greeks Alypius, Euclid, Ptolemy, and others have written excellent treatises on the subject. Of the Romans the distinguished Albinus has treated it with compendious brevity. We recall obtaining his book in a library in Rome and eagerly reading it. If this work has been carried off in consequence of the barbarian invasion, you have here the Latin version of Gaudentius by Mutianus; if you read this with close attention it will open to you the courts of this science. It is said that Apuleius of Madaura also has brought together the doctrines of this book in a Latin work. Our father Augustine, moreover, wrote six books on music, in which he showed that human speech naturally has rhythmical sounds and a measured harmony in its long and short syllables. And Censorinus has treated with subtlety the accents of our speech, declaring that they have a relation to the discipline of music. Of this book, among others, I have left a transcript with you.

8 Isidore of Seville

Isidore was born, probably, in the southeastern Spanish town of Cartagena between 560 and 564, and came to Seville in early childhood. After the death of his parents, he was raised by his brother Leander, bishop of Seville. He suceeded Leander in that office in about 600, and thereafter figured prominently in the life of the Visigothic church and court until his death in 636.

Isidore, like Boethius and Cassiodorus, served as a mediary between the classical and medieval cultures. His most important work is the *Twenty Books of Etymologies or Origins,* a massive encyclopedia of ancient ecclesiastical and secular learning and lore, written in his later years. Its immense influence in the Middle Ages is attested to by its preservation in more than one thousand manuscripts. Its notorious penchant for fanciful etymologies is well illustrated by the portion devoted to music, which is given below. Of musical interest also is the chapter on the liturgical offices (Book 6, Chapter 19).

FROM THE *Etymologies*

BOOK THREE

15. OF MUSIC AND ITS NAME

Music is the art of measurement consisting in tone and song. It is called music by derivation from the Muses. The Muses were so named ἀπὸ τοῦ μῶσθαι, that is, "from inquiring," because, as the ancients would have it, they inquired into the power of songs and the measurement of pitch. The sound of these, since it is a matter of impression upon the senses, flows by into the past and is left imprinted upon the memory. Hence it was fabled by the poets that the Muses were the daughters of Jove and Memory. Unless sounds are remembered by man, they perish, for they cannot be written down.[1]

TEXT: W. M. Lindsay, ed., *Isidori Hispalensis Episcopi Etymologiarum sive Originum libri XX* (Oxford, 1962), Book 3, chapters 15–23 (no pagination). Translation by William Strunk, Jr., and Oliver Strunk, revised by James McKinnon.

1. The last sentence of this passage is taken by many as evidence that musical notation was not known in Isidore's time. The passage as a whole appears to be a simplification of Augustine, *De ordine* 2.14: "And since what the intellect perceives (and numbers are manifestly of this class) is always of the present and is deemed immortal, while sound, since it is an impression upon the sense, flows by into the past and is imprinted upon the memory. Reason has permitted the poets to pretend, in a reasonable fable, that the Muses were the daughters of Jove and Memory. Hence this discipline, which addresses itself to the intellect and to the sense alike, has acquired the name of Music."

16. OF ITS INVENTORS

Moses says that the inventor of the art of music was Tubal, who was of the race of Cain, before the Flood.[2] The Greeks say that Pythagoras found its beginnings in the sound of hammers and the striking of stretched strings. Others report that Linus the Theban and Zetus and Amphion were the first to become illustrious in the art of music. After their time this discipline gradually came to be well ordered and was expanded in many ways, so that not to know music was as disgraceful as to be unlettered. It was not only introduced into sacred rites, but was used in all festivals and on all joyful or mournful occasions. For as hymns were sung in the worship of the gods, so hymenaeal songs were sung at weddings, and threnodies and lamentations to the sound of tibias at funerals. At banquets the lyre or the cithara was passed from hand to hand, and festal songs were assigned to each guest in turn.

17. WHAT MUSIC CAN DO

Thus without music no discipline can be perfect, for there is nothing without it. The very universe, it is said, is held together by a certain harmony of sounds, and the heavens themselves are made to revolve by the modulation of harmony. Music moves the feelings and changes the emotions. In battles, moreover, the sound of the trumpet rouses the combatants, and the more furious the trumpeting, the more valorous their spirit. A chant likewise encourages the rowers, music soothes the mind so that it can endure toil, and song assuages the weariness encountered in any task. Music also composes distraught minds, as may be read of David, who freed Saul from the unclean spirit by the art of melody. The very beasts also, even serpents, birds, and dolphins, are enticed by music to listen to her melody.[3] Indeed every word we speak, every pulsation of our veins, is related by musical rhythms to the powers of harmony.

18. OF THE THREE PARTS OF MUSIC[4]

The parts of music are three: harmonics, rhythmics, and metrics. Harmonics is that which distinguishes the high and low in sounds. Rhythmics is that which inquires whether words in combination sound well or badly together. Metrics is that which by valid reasoning knows the measures of the various metres; for example, the heroic, the iambic, and the elegiac.

19. OF THE THREEFOLD DIVISION OF MUSIC

Moreover for every sound which forms the material of songs, there is a threefold nature. The first is the harmonic, which consists of singing; the sec-

---

2. Genesis 4:21. On the topos of music's "inventors" see above, note 1 to the reading from Cassiodorus, p. 33.
3. See the reference to Varro in Cassiodorus's *Fundamentals* 5.8, p. 38.
4. See above, Cassiodorus, *Fundamentals* 5.5, p. 35.

ond, the organic, which is produced by blowing; the third, the rhythmic, in which the music is produced by the impulse of the fingers. For sound is caused either by the voice, as with the throat, or by blowing, as with the trumpet or the tibia, or by an impulse, as with the cithara or with anything else which becomes resonant when struck.[5]

20. OF THE FIRST DIVISION OF MUSIC, CALLED HARMONIC

The first division of music, which is called the harmonic, that is, the modulation of the voice, is the affair of comedians, tragedians, and choruses and of all who sing. It produces motion of the mind and body, and from this motion sound; from this sound comes the music which in man is called voice.

Voice is air struck *(verberatus)* by the breath, whence words *(verba)* also receive their name. Voice is proper to man and to irrational animals. But sound in other things is called voice by a misuse and not properly, as, "The voice of the trumpet snarled," and "Broken voices by the shore."[6] For the proper locutions are that the cliffs of the shore should resound, and, "The trumpet with resonant brass gave forth a terrible sound from afar."[7]

Harmony is a modulation of the voice and a concordance or mutual adaptation of several sounds. Symphony is a fusion of the modulation of low and high concordant sounds, produced either vocally or by blowing or striking. Through symphony low and high sounds are concordant, in such a way that if any one of them is dissonant it offends the sense of hearing. The opposite of this is diaphony, that is, discrepant or dissonant sounds. Euphony is sweetness of the voice; it is also called melody, from the word *mel* (honey), because of its sweetness.

Diastema is an interval of the voice composed of two or more sounds. Diesis consists of certain intervals and diminutions of modulation and interpolations between one sound and another.

Key *(tonus)* is a raised enunciation of the pitch. It is the categorization and ranking of the *harmoniae* according to the intonation or level of the voice. Musicians have divided the varieties of keys into fifteen, of which the Hyperlydian is the newest and highest, and the Hypodorian the lowest of all.

Song is an inflecting of the voice, for sound is simple and moreover it precedes song. Arsis is a lifting up of the voice, that is, a beginning. Thesis is a lowering of the voice, that is, an end.

---

5. See Augustine, *De ordine* 2.xiv: "Reason has understood that the judgment of the ear has to do only with sound and that sound has three varieties: it consists either in the voice of an animate being, or in what blowing produces in instruments, or in what is brought forth by striking. The first variety it understands to be the affair of tragedians, comedians, choruses, and the like, and in general of all who sing. The second it understands to be allotted to the auloi and similar instruments. To the third it understands to be given the citharas, lyres, cymbals, and anything else which becomes resonant when struck."

6. Vergil, *Aeneid* 3.556.

7. *Aeneid* 9.503.

Sweet voices are fine, full, clear, and high. Penetrating voices are those which can hold a note an unusually long time, in such a way that they continuously fill the entire area, like the sound of trumpets. A thin voice is one lacking in breath, as the voice of children or women or the sick. This is similar to strings, for the finest strings emit subtle, thin sounds.

In thick voices, as those of men, much breath is emitted at once. A sharp voice is high and thin, as we see in strings. A hard voice is one which emits sound violently, like thunder, or like the sound of an anvil whenever the hammer is struck against the hard iron. A harsh voice is a hoarse one, which is broken up by minute, dissimilar impulses. A blind voice is one which is choked off as soon as produced, and once silent cannot be prolonged, as is the case with crockery when struck.

A pretty (*vinnola*) voice is soft and flexible; it is so called from *vinnus*, a softly curling lock of hair. The perfect voice is high, sweet, and clear: high, to be adequate to the sublime; clear, to fill the ear; sweet, to soothe the minds of the hearers. If any one of these qualities is absent, the voice is not perfect.

21. OF THE SECOND DIVISION OF MUSIC, THE ORGANIC

The second division is the organic, found in the instruments which come to life and produce a musical pitch when filled by a stream of air, such as trumpets, reeds, pipes, organs, pandoria, and similar instruments. Organ is the generic name of all musical vessels. The Greeks have another name for the kind of organ to which bellows are applied, but their common custom is to call it the organ.

The trumpet was invented by the Etruscans, of whom Virgil wrote: "And the clangor of Etruscan trumpets resounded on high."[8] The trumpet was employed not only in battles, but in all festivals of special praise giving or rejoicing. Wherefore it is also said in the Psalter: "Sound the trumpet at the beginning of the month, and on the day of your great solemnity."[9] For the Jews were commanded to sound the trumpet at the time of the new moon, as they still do.

Tibias are said to have been devised in Phrygia. For a long time they were used only at funerals, but afterward in the sacred rites of the heathen as well. It is thought that they are called tibias because they were first made from the leg-bones of deer and fawns, and that then, by a misuse of the term, the name was used of those not made of legbones. Hence there is also the term *tibicen*, that is, the song of tibias.[10]

The reed is the name of a certain tree, called *calamus* from *calendo*, that is,

8. *Aeneid* 8.526.
9. Psalm 80(81):3.
10. Isidore is correct in deriving *tibicen* from *tibia* and *canere* (to sing), but the term is properly applied to the player not the song itself.

giving out voice. The pipe some think to have been invented by Mercury; others, by Faunus, whom the Greeks call Pan; others by Daphnis, a shepherd of Agrigentum in Sicily. The pipe (*fistula*) is also named from sending forth a sound, for in Greek voice is called φῶς, and sent forth, στόλια.

The sambuca, among musicians, is a type of drum.[11] The word means a kind of fragile wood, from which tibias are made. The pandoria is named from its inventor, of whom Virgil says: "Pan first taught men to join reeds together with wax; Pan cares for sheep and for shepherds."[12] For among the heathen he was the god of shepherds, who first adapted reeds of unequal length to music and fitted them together with studious art.

22. OF THE THIRD DIVISION OF MUSIC, WHICH IS CALLED RHYTHMIC

The third division is the rhythmic, having to do with strings and striking, to which are assigned the different species of cithara, also the tympanum, the cymbal, the sistrum, vessels of bronze and silver, others whose hard metal yields an agreeable clanging when struck, and other instruments of this nature.[13]

Tubal, as was said before, is regarded as the inventor of the cithara and psaltery, but by the Greeks Apollo was believed to have first discovered the use of the cithara. According to their tradition, the form of the cithara was originally like that of the human chest, it received its name because it gives forth sound as the chest gives forth voice. In Doric, moreover, the chest was called κιθάρα. Gradually numerous species were invented, as psalteries, lyres, barbitons, phoenices, and pektises, and those which are called Indian citharas and are played by two musicians at once; also many others, some of square and others of triangular form. The number of strings was also increased and the shape altered. The ancients called the cithara *fidicula* and *fidicen*, because the strings are in good accord with each other, as befits men among whom there is trust (*fides*).[14]

The ancient cithara had seven strings; whence Virgil's phrase, "the seven distinctions of pitch,"[15] "distinctions" because no string gives the same note as its neighbor. There were seven strings because that number filled the range of the voice, and because the heavens sound with seven motions. The strings (*chordae*) are so called from *cor* (heart), because the striking of the strings of the cithara is like the beating of the heart in the breast. Mercury was their inventor; he was the first to draw sound from strings.

11. Here Isidore is simply wrong; the ancient sambuca was a kind of harp.
12. *Eclogues* 2.32.
13. Note the inclusion here within the same category of what we moderns distinguish as strings and percussion.
14. A good example of the fanciful sort of etymology for which Isidore's work is so well known.
15. *Aeneid* 6.646.

The psaltery, popularly called *canticum,* has its name from *psallendo* (singing), because the chorus answers its voice in consonance. It resembles a barbaric cithara in the form of the letter delta, but there is this difference between it and the cithara, that it has its wooden sound-box above, and the strings are struck below and sound above, while the cithara has the soundbox below. The Hebrews used a ten-stringed psaltery, because of the Ten Commandments of their law.

The lyre is so called ἀπὸ τοῦ ληρεῖν (from sounding folly), that is, from the variety of voices, because it produces dissimilar sounds. They say it was invented by Mercury in the following manner. When the Nile, retreating into its channels, had left various animals in the fields, a tortoise was among them. After it had putrefied and its sinews remained stretched within its shell, it gave out a sound on being struck by Mercury. He fashioned the lyre using this model and gave it to Orpheus, who applied himself studiously to it and is deemed not merely to have swayed wild beasts with his art, but to have moved rocks and forests with the measures of his song. Musicians have claimed in their fables that the lyre was placed among the constellations because of his love of study and the glory of his song.

The tympanum is a skin or hide stretched over one side of a wooden frame; it is a half-drum, shaped like a sieve. It is called tympanum because it is a half, for which reason a half-pearl is called a tympanum. It, like the drum, is struck with a stick. Cymbals are certain vessels which produce sound when struck together. They are called cymbals because they are struck together in time with dancing, since the Greeks call dancing συμβαλεῖν.

The sistrum is named from its inventress, for Isis, a queen of the Egyptians, is considered to have invented this species of instrument. Juvenal has: "Let Isis with angry sistrum blind my eyes."[16] Women use this instrument because a woman invented it. Among the Amazons the army of women was summoned to battle by the sistrum. The bell *(tintinnabulum)* is named from its sound, as are also the clapping *(plausus)* of hands and the creaking *(stridor)* of hinges. Drum *(symphonia)* is the ordinary name of a wooden frame covered on both sides with stretched skin, which the musicians strike in one place and another with small sticks; and there results a most delightful sound from the concord of low and high.

23. OF MUSICAL NUMBERS

You obtain musical numbers in this manner. Having set down the extreme terms, as say 6 and 12, you see by how many units 12 exceeds 6, and it is by 6 units. You square this: 6 times 6 is 36. You then add together those first extremes, 6 and 12; together they make 18. You then divide 36 by 18, which gives 2. Add this to the smaller number, that is, 6; this will give 8, which will be the harmonic mean between 6 and 12. From this it appears that 8 exceeds

16. *Satires* 13.931.

6 by 2 units, that is, by one third of 6, and 8 is exceeded by 12 by 4 units, one third of 12. By the same fraction that it exceeds, it is exceeded.[17]

But just as this ratio appears in the universe from the revolution of the spheres, so in the microcosm it is so inexpressibly potent that the man without its perfection and deprived of its harmony does not exist. And by the perfection of the same music, measures consist of arsis and thesis, that is, of raising and lowering.

17. This method for finding the harmonic mean between two extremes will give the correct answer only when the greater term is twice the lesser. Isidore's error lies in directing that the difference between the extremes be squared. It must be multiplied by the lesser term. With this correction, his method agrees with that given by Boethius, *The Fundamentals of Music* 2.17: "If we seek the harmonic mean, we add the extremes, for example 10 and 40, one to another, making 50. Their difference, which is 30, we multiply by the lesser term, that is 10, making 10 times 30, or 300. This we divide by 50, making 6. This we add to the lesser term, making 16. If now we place this number between 10 and 40, we have a harmonic proportion."

CHANT AND LITURGY IN THE EARLY MIDDLE AGES

9 St. Benedict of Nursia

St. Benedict was born to a prosperous family in the region of Nursia, near Spoleto, sometime in the later decades of the fifth century. As a young man, he cut short his education in Rome to devote himself to the monastic life. After a period of several years at Subiaco, east of Rome, spent at times in solitude and at other times in attempts at monastic organization, he journeyed south to Monte Cassino, a prominent hill near the town of Cassinum, halfway between Rome and Naples. Here he founded the monastery that would come to be looked upon as the mother house of Western monasticism. He died sometime after a meeting with the Gothic leader Totila in 546.

Benedict's significance lies in his Rule, which he composed for the community at Monte Cassino. Recommended by its clarity and reasonableness, it progressed from its obscure origins to become institutionalized during the Carolingian period as the universally observed Western monastic rule. Many would claim it to be the single most influential document written in the Middle Ages. Of musical relevance are the chapters, translated below, that describe the monastic Office.

FROM THE *Rule of St. Benedict*

VIII. CONCERNING THE DIVINE OFFICE AT NIGHT

In wintertime, that is, from the first of November until Easter, it seems reasonable to arise at the eighth hour of the night,[1] so that the brethren do so with a moderately full sleep after midnight and with their digestion completed. And whatever time remains after Vigils[2] should be devoted to the study of the psalms and lessons by those brothers who lack sufficient knowledge of them. And from Easter, in turn, to the first of November, let the hour of rising be postponed so that Lauds, which are celebrated as the light of day sets in, are separated from Vigils by a brief interval in which the brothers may attend to the necessities of nature.

TEXT: Adalbert de Vogüé, *La Règle de Saint Benoît*, vol. 2, Sources Chrétiennes 182 (Paris, 1972), pp. 508–36. Translation by James McKinnon.

1. Benedict's Rule follows the Roman *horarium*, which divides the day into twelve daylight hours and twelve night hours. During the winter, night hours are longer than daylight hours, while the opposite is true for the summer. At the latitude of Monte Cassino, a midwinter night hour is approximately one hour and twenty minutes of modern clock time. Thus Benedict's eighth hour of the night, two hours after midnight, would be about 2:40 A.M. on December 21. The summer time adjustments that Benedict calls for later in this chapter and in Chapter 10 are required by the shorter night hours of the summer.
2. Benedict's nighttime office, *vigiliae*, the equivalent of the misnamed medieval Matins, is translated "Vigils" here; while the service of morning praise, Benedict's *matutini*, is translated "Lauds."

IX. How Many Psalms Are to Be Said at the Night Offices

. In the aforesaid wintertime, let there first be said, three times, the verse "O Lord, open thou my lips, and my mouth shall proclaim thy praise";[3] this is followed by Psalm 3 with the *Gloria* [*patri*] and after this Psalm 94 to be sung with the antiphon, or in any case to be sung. There follows next the Ambrosian hymn; then six psalms with antiphons. When these have been said,[4] and the versicle as well, let the abbot give the blessing. And after all are seated upon the benches three lessons are to be read in turn by brothers from the codex on the lectern, with three responsories sung between the lessons. Two of the responsories are to be sung without the *Gloria* but after the third lesson, whoever sings adds the *Gloria* and as soon as the singer begins this, all should rise from their seats out of honor and reverence for the Holy Trinity. The books to be read at Vigils are those with the divine authority of both Old and New Testaments, as well as commentaries upon them, that were composed by recognized and orthodox catholic Fathers. After these three readings with their responsories, there should follow the remaining six psalms to be sung with *Alleluia;* and after these the reading of the Apostle[5] recited by heart, a versicle, and the litany, that is, the *Kyrie eleison.* In this manner are the nocturnal Vigils to be brought to a close.

X. How the Nocturnal Praise Is to Be Said in the Summer Time

From Easter to the first of November the same number of psalms as given above is to be maintained, although the lessons are not to be read from the codex because of the brevity of the night hours. In place of the three lessons one from the New Testament is to be recited from memory; this is followed by a brief responsory. And all the rest is done as described above, that is, never less than twelve psalms are to be recited at the nightly vigils, not counting Psalms 3 and 94.

XI. How Vigils Are to Be Said on Sundays

On the Lord's day we must rise earlier for Vigils. The following order should be observed in these Vigils: after the six aforementioned psalms and the versicle have been sung, and all are seated in proper order, the four lessons are to be read from the codex with their responsories, according to what we have said

3. Psalm 1:17.
4. The Latin *dicere* (to say) is translated here either "to say" or "to recite," while only *cantare* (to sing) is translated "to sing" or "to chant." But by no means is this meant to imply that psalms, which were in Benedict's language "said," were not in fact sung or chanted. In Early Christian literature *dicere* is used interchangeably with *cantare* in connection with the singing of psalms.
5. The term "Apostle," although referring specifically to St. Paul, is a generic early Christian term for a reading from the New Testament epistles.

above; the singer chants the *Gloria* only for the fourth responsory, and as soon as he begins it all should arise out of reverence. After these lessons the same order is followed: six more psalms with antiphons, and the versicle. Again four other lessons with their responsories are to be read following the above order. After these three canticles from the Prophets, selected by the abbot, are to chanted; these are sung with *Alleluia.* When the versicle has been recited, and the abbot has given the blessing, four other lessons, these from the New Testament, are to be read following the above order. But after the fourth responsory the abbot intones the hymn *Te deum laudamus.* When this is completed the abbot reads the lesson from the Gospel book, as all stand in awe and reverence. When this has been read let all respond *Amen,* and immediately the abbot follows with the hymn *Te decet laus;* then after he gives the blessing let them begin Lauds.

This order of Vigils is always to be observed on the Lord's day whether it be summer or winter, unless somehow the brothers should happen to arise late, in which case the lessons and responsories are to be shortened. We should take care that this does not happen, but if it does, he by whose neglect it came about, must make due satisfaction to God in the oratorio.

XII. HOW THE OFFICE OF LAUDS IS TO BE CELEBRATED

Let Sunday Lauds begin with Psalm 66 said straight through[6] without antiphon. Then let Psalm 50 be recited with *Alleluia,* and after this Psalms 117 and 62; then the *Benedicite*[7] and the *Laudate* psalms,[8] one lesson by heart from the Apocalypse with responsory, an Ambrosian hymn, the versicle, the Gospel canticle, the litany—and all is done.

XIII. HOW LAUDS ARE TO BE SAID ON WEEKDAYS

On weekdays Lauds should be said in this way: let Psalm 66 be recited without antiphon, drawn out somewhat as on Sunday, so that all are assembled for Psalm 50, which is recited with antiphon. After this two other psalms are to be recited according to custom, that is, on Monday Psalms 5 and 35, on Tuesday Psalms 42 and 56, on Wednesdays Psalms 63 and 64, and on Thursday Psalms 87 and 89, on Friday Psalms 75 and 91, and on Saturday Psalm 142 and the canticle from Deuteronomy,[9] which is to be divided into two sections, each with closing *Gloria.* On the other days let a canticle from the Prophets be

6. Benedict's *in directum* is translated here as "straight through," that is, the psalm is sung straight through without the addition of antiphons.
7. *Benedicite* is the canticle of the three youths in the fiery furnace; it appears in Daniel 3:52–90 (but only in the Greek-Latin-Catholic textual tradition, not the Hebrew-Protestant).
8. The *Laudate* psalms, Psalms 148–50, were associated with Lauds from its Early Christian origins and give the service its name; they are so called because of their theme of praise; the first and last of them, in point of fact, begin with the word *laudate.*
9. The second canticle of Moses, *Audite coeli,* Deuteronomy 32.1–43.

recited, one proper to each day, as they are sung in the church of Rome. After this the *Laudate* psalms are to follow, then a lesson from the Apostle to be said by heart, a responsory, an Ambrosian hymn, a versicle, a Gospel canticle, the litany—and all is done.

Certainly the morning and evening offices must never be allowed to conclude without the prior saying the entire Lord's Prayer within the hearing of all, this, because of the thorns of contention that are liable to arise among the brethren; thus bound by the pledge that they give in this prayer, "Forgive us as we forgive," they purge themselves from this sort of failing. At the other offices only the last part of the prayer is to be said, so that all can respond, "But deliver us from evil."

XIV. How Vigils Are to Be Said on the Festivals of the Saints

On the festivals of the saints and on all other solemn occasions, the Office should be performed as we described it for Sundays, except that psalms, antiphons, and lessons that are appropriate to the day are to be selected; the overall manner of execution, however, as given above, should be maintained.

XV. At What Times the Alleluia Should Be Said

The *Alleluia* is to be said after both psalms and responsories, from the sacred Pasch to Pentecost without interruption. But from Pentecost to the beginning of Lent let it be said each night at the Nocturns only with the second group of six psalms. On every Sunday outside Lent let the canticles of Vigils and Lauds, and the psalms of Lauds, Prime, Terce, Sext, and None be sung with *Alleluia;* but at Vespers let there be an antiphon. Responsories, however, are never chanted with *Alleluia,* except from Easter to Pentecost.

XVI. How the Work of God Is to Be Performed throughout the Day

As the Prophet says: "Seven times during the day I have spoken thy praise."[10] This sacred number of seven is thus observed by us if we fulfil the obligations of our service at Lauds, Prime, Terce, Sext, None, Vespers, and Compline; since he says of these day hours, "Seven times during the day I have spoken thy praise." And of the nightly Vigils the very same prophet says: "I arose in the middle of the night to confess thee."[11] Therefore let us render praise to our Creator "for his just judgments" at these hours, that is, Lauds, Prime, Terce, Sext, None, Vespers, and Compline; and at night let us arise to confess him.

10. Psalm 118(119):164.
11. Psalm 118(119):62.

XVII. How Many Psalms Are to Be Said at These Hours

We have already established the order of psalmody at Vigils and Matins; now let us see to the remaining hours. At Prime three psalms should be sung, one by one, and not with only a single *Gloria;* the hymn for this hour comes after the verse *Deus in adjutorium,* before the psalms are begun. At the completion of the three psalms, let one lesson be read, then the versicle, the Kyrie eleison, and the dismissal. At Terce, Sext, and None, the same order of prayer is to be observed, that is, the hymn appropriate to the hour, three psalms, a lesson and versicle, Kyrie eleison, and the concluding prayers. If a larger group is present, the psalms are to be said with antiphons, but if a smaller one, they are sung straight through.

Let the service of Vespers be limited to four psalms with antiphons; after these psalms a lesson is to be read, then a responsory, an Ambrosian hymn, a versicle, a Gospel canticle, the litany, and the Lord's Prayer by way of conclusion. Compline is to be limited to the recitation of three psalms which are said straight through without antiphon; after these there follow the hymn of the hour, a lesson, a versicle, the *Kyrie eleison,* and by way of conclusion the blessing.

XVIII. In What Order the Psalms Are to Be Said

First let there be said the verse, "O God, incline thee to my aid, O Lord make haste to help me";[12] then the hymn appropriate to the hour. Then at Prime on Sunday, four chapters of Psalm 118 are to be said, and at the remaining hours, Terce, Sext, and None, three chapters each of the aforesaid Psalm 118. At Prime on Monday let three psalms be said, that is, Psalms 1, 2, and 6. And thus for each day at Prime, until Sunday, let three psalms be said in order up to Psalm 19, with Psalms 9 and 17 divided into two parts. And thus it happens that Sunday Vigils is always to begin with Psalm 20.

On Monday the remaining nine chapters of Psalm 118 should be said at Terce, Sext, and None, three at each hour. With Psalm 118 completed, then, in two days (Sunday and Monday), on Tuesday three psalms should be said at Terce, at Sext, and at None—Psalms 119 to 127, a total of nine. These psalms are always to be repeated in the same way at the same hours until Sunday; and the same arrangement of hymns, lessons, and versicles should be maintained for every day. Thus Sunday Prime will always begin with Psalm 118.

Vespers is to be sung every day with the chanting of four psalms. These should begin with Psalm 109 and extend to Psalm 147, omitting those which have been reserved for particular offices, namely, Psalms 117 to 127, and Psalms 133 and 142; all the rest should be sung at Vespers. And because there are three psalms too few, those of the aforesaid group that are longer should be divided, that is, Psalms 138, 143, and 144. But because Psalm 116 is short,

12. Psalm 69(70):2.

it should be joined to Psalm 115. With the order of Vesper psalms thus arranged, the rest of the service as determined above is to be completed, that is, the lesson, the responsory, the hymn, the versicle, and the canticle. At Compline the same psalms are to be repeated every day, namely, Psalms 4, 90, and 133.

The order of the daily psalmody thus arranged, all remaining psalms are to be distributed equally over the seven nightly Vigils; twelve can be assigned each night by dividing the longer psalms. We strongly recommend that whoever is not pleased with this distribution of the psalms, should arrange them in some other way that he considers to be better. But in any event let him see to it that every week the complete Psalter with its one hundred and fifty psalms is sung, always starting from the beginning at Sunday Vigils. For monks who sing less than the Psalter with its customary canticles in the course of a week display a lack of dedication and devotion, whereas we read of our holy fathers who arduously fulfilled in a single day what we tepid souls accomplish in an entire week.

XIX. ON THE DISCIPLINE OF PSALMODY

We believe that God is present everywhere and that "the eyes of the Lord look upon good men and evil in every place";[13] but we must believe without a shadow of doubt that this is especially so when we assist at the Divine Office. Let us always be mindful, then, of what the Prophet says: "Serve the Lord in fear";[14] and again, "Sing psalms wisely";[15] and, "I will sing to thee in the sight of the angels."[16] Hence we must consider how we are to comport ourselves in the sight of the Divinity and of his angels; and we must be thus instant in psalmody that our mind and voice are in harmony.

13. Proverbs 15:3.
14. Psalm 2:11.
15. Psalm 46:8 (the phrase appears only in the Greek-Latin text tradition).
16. Psalm 137.1.

10 Pseudo-Germanus

The "Exposition of the Ancient Gallican Liturgy" is the first of two letters formerly attributed to St. Germanus of Paris (d. 576). That they are considerably later is suggested by their apparent reliance upon the writings of Isidore of Seville (d. 636). Most scholars now believe them to have originated in the early eighth century somewhere in Burgundy, perhaps at Autun, where the manuscript containing them has long resided. (A. van der Mensbrugghe continues to argue for their authenticity in his "Pseudo-Germanus Reconsidered," *Studia Patristica*, vol. 5 [Texte und Arbeiten no. 80, 1962]: 172–84). The first letter, translated here, is a colorful explanation of the Gallican Mass in the style of allegorical exegesis. Although the central concern of the letter is clearly the symbolic significance of the liturgy, it is possible to extract from its text a fairly precise description of the various chants and ritual events that are the subject of its fanciful interpretations. The description refers, in all probability, to the Gallican Mass of only one time and place, perhaps Autun in the early eighth century, but it conforms in its more general features to what we know from other descriptive references to Gallican services (see William S. Porter, *The Gallican Rite* [London: 1958]). Most noteworthy is the dependence of the rite upon Eastern liturgies and the affinity with the contemporary Mozarabic Mass. The Gallican tendency to employ Ordinary hymnic chants stands in sharp contrast to Rome's use of Proper psalmic chants.

Exposition of the Ancient Gallican Liturgy

PREFACE. The Mass, first and greatest of spiritual gifts, is sung in commemoration of the Lord's death; the death of Christ becomes the life of the world, so that by this offering the salvation of the living and the eternal rest of the departed are secured.

1. BEFORE THE READINGS. The antiphon[1] before the readings is sung as a representation of those patriarchs, who before the Flood proclaimed the coming of Christ in mystic voices; like Enoch, of the seventh generation from Adam, who lifted up by God prophesied: "Behold the Lord cometh with thousands of his saints to exercize justice." The Apostle Jude, brother of James, preserves this testimony in his epistle.[2]

And just as in the prophesies of the patriarchs the hand of the Lord came over the Ark to withhold the fruits of the sacrifice from the evil ones, so too, as the clergy sings, the priest, in the image of Christ, proceeds from the sacristy, as if from heaven, into the Ark of the Lord, which is the Church, in order that, as much by encouragement as by warning, he may nourish good works among the people and root out evil.

2. THE SILENCE. The deacon proclaims the silence for two reasons, so that a quiet congregation may better hear the word of God, and so that our hearts may be deaf to any impure thoughts and thus better welcome the word of God.

3. The priest, then, blesses the people saying this, "The Lord be always with you." And he in turn is blessed by all, who reply, "And with thy spirit," He is

---

TEXT: Edward. C. Ratcliff, ed., *Expositio Antiquae Liturgiae Gallicanae* (London: Henry Bradshaw Society, 1971). Translation by James McKinnon.

1. There is no hint as to the character of this antiphon, except for the circumstance that it was sung by the clergy during the entrance of the celebrant.
2. Jude 14.

thus that much more worthy to bless the people since by the grace of God he receives a blessing from the mouth of the entire congregation.

4. THE AIUS.[3] The *Aius* is sung before the "Prophecy" in the Greek language for this reason: because the proclamation of the New Testament proceeded into the world through the Greek tongue, except for the Apostle Matthew, who was the first in Judea to compose the gospel of Christ in the Hebrew language. Thus was preserved the honor of the tongue which first took the gospel of Christ to its bosom, and which taught the first canticle in its literature. With the presiding priest[4] intoning, the church sings the *Aius,* chanting in Latin along with Greek,[5] so as to manifest the union of Old and New Testaments. The Amen that is recited is from the Hebrew, like that title which Pilate placed over the cross, at God's prompting in a trinity of languages, "Jesus of Nazareth, king of the Jews," thus proclaiming, while ignorant of the fact, that he was indeed the holy king.

5. The three boys who next sing the Kyrie eleison three times as from one mouth, do so as a representation of the threefold language of sacred law— Hebrew, Greek, and Latin—and after the three ages of the world, that is, before the Law, under the Law, and under the dispensation of grace.

6. THE PROPHECY [the *Benedictus*]. The canticle of Zachary the high priest is sung in honor of St. John the Baptist. For the beginning of salvation consists in the sacrament of baptism, which John received as his ministry from a generous God; and as the shadow of the Old Law receded and the brightness of the new Gospel emerged, John, intermediating as last of the prophets and first of the evangelists, shone as a lamp, indeed, before the face of the light. Thus the Church sings in alternate voices the "Prophecy" which his father sang at the news of his birth.

7. THE PROPHET AND THE APOSTLE [the Old Testament reading and the Epistle]. The prophetic reading, that of the Old Testament, maintains its place, chastising evil and announcing the future, so that we may understand that the God who thundered in prophecy is the very same who taught in the Apostle and who shone forth in the splendor of the Gospel. For what the Prophet says is to come, the Apostle teaches as already accomplished. The Acts of the Apostles and the Apocalypse of John are read for the renewal of Paschal rejoicing, maintaining the order of the calendar, just as the Old Testament histories are read in the Pentecostal season, and the acts of the holy confessors and martyrs on their festivals, so that the people will understand how greatly Christ, in

3. *Aius,* literally Greek for "holy." The *Aius* is the celebrated Trisagion chant, "Holy God, mighty God, holy immortal one, have mercy on us," that was sung in the Latin medieval liturgy only during the adoration of the cross on Good Friday. It was regularly sung in most Eastern liturgies, as here, before the readings.

4. *Praesul* is translated here "presiding priest," literally, in classical Latin, one who dances at the head of a procession; an equally plausible translation might be "cantor."

5. In the Western version of the chant, the Latin translation is interspersed after each phrase of the Greek; see the *Liber Usualis,* p. 705.

granting a sign of virtue to a servant, loved him whom the pious faithful claim as their patron.

8. THE HYMN [the *Benedicite* of the three youths]. The hymn of the three youths is sung following the readings as a representation of the holy ancients, who sitting in darkness, awaited the coming of the Lord. And just as a fourth being, an angel, joined the youths as they sang and overcame the flames with a cloud of dew;[6] so too did that very son of God, the angel of the great counsel, join those who awaited the messiah, and, breaking the rule of Tartarus and setting them free, brought them the joy of the resurrection, as the evangelist teaches.[7]

9. And for this reason the Church maintains an order of service in which no Collect is inserted between the hymn of the youths (*Benedictio*) and the gospel, but only the response (*Responsurium*),[8] which is sung by children as a representation of those Innocents whose deaths as companions of Christ in birth, are narrated in the gospel,[9] or of those children who cried out to the Lord in the temple, "Hosanna to the Son of David," as he drew near to his Passion— as the psalmist declares, "Out of the mouth of infants and of sucklings you have perfected praise."[10]

10. THE AIUS BEFORE THE GOSPEL. Then in anticipation of the holy gospel a cleric sings the *Aius* again with a clear voice, after the image of the angels at the gates of hell who cried out before the face of Christ: "Lift up your gates, ye princes, and ye the eternal gates shall be lifted up, and the Lord of powers, the king of glory, shall enter in."[11]

11. THE GOSPEL. The procession with the holy gospel book goes out, like the power of the triumphant Christ from death, with the melodies spoken of above [the *Aius*] and with seven lighted candelabras, which are the seven gifts of the Holy Spirit or the seven lights of the Law affixed to the mystery of the cross. The procession mounts the ambo, as if it were Christ attaining the seat of his royal Father, so that from there he might proclaim the gifts of life, while the clergy cries out, "Glory be to thee, O Lord," as a representation of the angels who appeared to the shepherds at the birth of the Lord and sang, "Glory to God in the highest."

12. THE SANCTUS AFTER THE GOSPEL. The Sanctus,[12] which is sung as the gospel book is returned, is chanted by a cleric as a representation of the saints who, following Jesus Christ as he returned from hell, sang a canticle of praise,[13]

---

6. See Daniel 3:49–50.
7. See the apocryphal Gospel of Nicodemus.
8. This would appear to be a responsorial psalm, in all probability the equivalent of the Roman gradual psalm.
9. See Matthew 2.16.
10. See Matthew 21.15–16.
11. Psalm 23.7.
12. This is the *Aius* in Latin, not the Sanctus that follows the Preface.
13. See the Gospel of Nicodemus.

or of the four and twenty elders commemorated by John in the Apocalypse, who cast down their crowns before the Lamb and sang a sweet song.[14]

13. THE HOMILIES. The homilies of the holy fathers that are read are substituted for the preaching of an individual, so that whatever the Prophet, the Apostle, or the gospel advised, this doctor or shepherd of the Church would relate to the people in plainer speech, exercizing his art so that neither crudity of language would offend the learned nor honorable eloquence become obscure to the simple.

14. THE PRAYER. The chanting of the Prayer by deacons (levitas) had its origin in the Books of Moses, so that the deacons, after the preaching had been heard by the people, should pray for the people, and the priests, prostrate before the Lord, should intercede for the sins of the people. As the Lord said to Aaron: "You and your sons and all the tribe of Levi shall bear the sins of my people."[15]

15. THE CATECHUMENS. The deacon cries aloud, according to the ancient ritual of the Church, that the catechumens must go outside. So Jews as well as heretics and pagans under instruction, who, once proud, have come to be baptized and before that to be examined, should stay in the church to hear the counsel of the Old and New Testaments, after which the deacons pray for them, and the priest recites a collect after the prayer. But finally they must go out through the doors because they are not worthy to stay in the church while the sacrifice is offered. And outside before the entrance, prostrate on the earth, they should listen to the telling of God's wonders. This task falls to the deacon or the ostiary, for just as he should admonish them to go outside, he should see to it that no one unworthy lingers in the church. As the Lord says: "Give not that which is holy to dogs, and do not cast your pearls before the swine."[16] For what is holier on earth than to prepare the body and blood of Christ, and what more unclean than the dogs and pigs that provide an image for the person who has neither been cleansed by baptism nor fortified with the sign of the cross?

16. We are enjoined, in the spiritual sense, to stand at the entrance and to observe silence, that is, so that free from the confusion of words and vices we may place the sign of the cross before our face, lest concupiscence enter through the eyes or anger through the ear, or lest shameful speech pass through the lips; and let the heart pay heed to this alone, that it receive Christ unto itself.

17. THE SONUM [the Offertory chant]. The Sonum is that which is sung during the procession of the offerings.[17] It has its origin in this: the Lord com-

14. See the Book of Revelation 4:10–11.
15. See Numbers 18:23.
16. Matthew 7:6.
17. The elaborate procession described here, that brings in the eucharistic elements of bread and wine (referring to them as "body" and "blood" in anticipation of their consecration), is very similar to the Byzantine Great Entrance. Likewise the Gallican chant, the Sonum, would appear to be the celebrated Cherubicon Hymn, which was sung during the Great Entrance;

manded Moses to make trumpets of silver that the Levites would blow during the offering of the victim, and this would be a sign by which the people would understand at what hour the sacrifice would take place; and all would bow down and adore the Lord, until there appeared that column of fire and cloud that blessed the offering.[18] Now, however, the Church hymns with sweet melody the body of Christ as it approaches the altar, not with blameless[19] trumpets, but with spiritual voices proclaiming the brilliant wonders of Christ.

18. The body of the Lord is carried within towers,[20] because the tomb of the Lord was cut into the rock in the form of a tower, and within was the funeral couch where the body of the Lord rested, and whence he, the king of glory, arose in triumph. The blood of Christ, in particular, is offered in a chalice[21] because in such a vessel the mystery of the Eucharist was consecrated "on the day before he suffered," as he said himself, "this is the chalice of my blood, the mystery of faith which is poured out for many unto the remission of sins."[22]

．　　．　　．　　．　　．

20. [Conclusion of the *Sonum*]. The *Laudes* are the Alleluia which John in the Apocalypse heard sung in the heavens after the resurrection of Christ.[23] Therefore at that moment when the body of the Lord is covered by the pallium, just as Christ is covered by the heavens, the Church is wont to sing the angelic song, which has a first, second, and third *alleluia*, signifying the three ages: before the Law, under the Law, and under grace.

．　　．　　．　　．　　．

22. [The Kiss of Peace]. They extend the Peace of Christ to each other so that by a mutual kiss they may retain in themselves a sense of charity, and so that any discord might fade away and quickly revert to friendship and so that one might seek forgiveness from his neighbor and not, by giving a false Peace, achieve a traitorous relationship. And the reception of the Eucharist and the bestowal of the blessing will be all the more beneficial to the extent that Christ

---

the Cherubicon, like the Sonum, is an "angelic song," and it concludes in one version, as does the Sonum, with three *alleluias* (see paragraph 20 below).

18. A confused reminiscence of several Old Testament descriptions of sacrifice; see, for example, Numbers 10:2–10, Numbers 14:14, and Ecclesiasticus 50:19–20.

19. "Blameless" *(irreprensibilis)* trumpets would seem to refer to the circumstance that patristic authors found it necessary to justify God's allowing of the ancient Hebrews to use musical instruments at sacrifice; see McKinnon, *Music in Early Christian Literature*, items 173, 174, 229, 230, 231, and 232.

20. The bread is carried in a vessel fashioned in the likeness of a tower.

21. The wine, carried in a chalice, follows the bread in the procession.

22. The quotation is from the prayer of consecration, apparently the same as that of the Roman rite. Omitted from the remainder of the translation are several short paragraphs that refer to certain eucharistic vessels and cloths and to the consecration of the bread and wine that is to follow later in the service.

23. Book of Revelation 19:1–6.

sees their hearts to be at peace; for it was he himself who gave this commandment to his disciples before his ascension into the heavens: "My peace I leave
with you, my peace I give to you. I give you a new commandment, that you
love one another, and in this will all recognize that you are my disciples, if you
love one another."[24]

23. [The Preface]. "Lift up your hearts." Thus the priest admonishes that no
worldly considerations are to remain in our breasts. At the hour of the holy
sacrifice Christ will be that much the better received in the mind to the extent
that one's thoughts strive to fix upon him alone.

24a. [The Fraction]. The fraction and mingling of the body of the Lord was
manifested in ancient times to the holy fathers as an extraordinary mystery: as
the priest broke up the offering he appeared to be an angel of God who cut up
with a knife the limbs of a shining youth and caught his blood in the chalice,
so that they would believe the word of the Lord to be true when he said his
flesh was food and his blood was drink.[25]

24b. By this fraction the priest wishes to multiply the bread, and likewise he
adds [to the wine] so that heavenly things are mixed with earthly.[26] As the
priest prays the heavens are opened, and as he breaks the bread a suppliant
cleric sings the antiphon[27] because while the Lord endured the death agony all
the elements of the trembling earth joined in testimony.[28]

25. [The Lord's Prayer]. The Lord's Prayer is said, moreover, so that all of
our prayer is included within the prayer of the Lord.

26. [The Blessing]. The Lord commanded through Moses that the Blessing
of the People should be dispensed by the priests: "Say to Aaron and to his sons,
'Thus will you bless my people, *The Lord bless you and keep you, etc.*' "[29]

Aaron thus took the place of the bishop and his sons took the place of the
priests; the Lord therefore commanded both to bless the people, yet in order
to preserve the honor of the pontiff the sacred canons have ordained that the
bishop should give the longer blessing. And the priest should dispense the
shorter blessing in these words: "May the peace, faith, and love, and the communion of the body and blood of our Lord Jesus Christ be always with you." It
is allowed, then, that the priest give this blessing which God dictated to Moses,
and no one can contradict him because the Lord said: "Heaven and earth will
pass away, but my words will not pass away."[30] And for this reason is the bless-

---

24. John, 13:34–35.
25. There is a reference here to a curious episode told in the *Vitae Patrum* (Jacques Migne, ed.,
    Patrologia cursus completus, series latina, vol. 73, cols. 978–79); the vision of the slain boy was
    supposed to have converted a certain monk who had doubted the Real Presence.
26. By breaking the bread the priest multiplies it for distribution at Communion, and similarly he
    adds unconsecrated wine to the consecrated.
27. An antiphon of unknown character, not, in all probability, the Agnus dei, which was introduced
    at the Fraction of the Roman Mass only shortly before 700. The following reference to the
    trembling earth at Christ's death may offer a hint as to the content of its text.
28. See Matthew 27:51.
29. Numbers 6:22–27.
30. Luke 21:33; Mark 13:31.

ing given before the communion, so that the mystery of blessedness shall enter into a blessed vessel.

27. Christ shows how sweet is the sacred communion of soul and body in the words of the evangelist: "If you abide in me and my words abide in you, whatever you will ask the Father in my name shall be done for you."[31]

28. [The Communion chant]. The *Trecanum*[32] which is sung is a sign of the catholic faith. Proceding from a belief in the Trinity, its first part revolves to the second, its second to the third, then its third back to the second, and the second again to the first, just as in the mystery of the Trinity the Father is embraced within the Son, the Son within the Holy Spirit, and in return the Holy Spirit within the Son, and the Son again in the Father.

And now concludes the epistle in which the solemn liturgical order, briefly explained, is presented.

31. John 15:7.
32. The *Trecanum* is an unidentified Trinitarian chant. Johannes Quasten suggests that it might have been "The Holy Thing to the Holies," which is sung at this point in several Eastern liturgies; see his "Oriental Influence in the Gallican Liturgy," *Traditio* 1 (1943): 78.

11 Anonymous (8th Century)

Ordo romanus XVII is one of some fifty documents, the *Ordines romani,* that describe the papal liturgy of eighth-century Rome and its adaptation by the Franks. It was composed by an East Frankish monk sometime during the last two decades of the eighth century. Consisting of various liturgical prescriptions for the Mass and Office that cover the entire church year from Advent to the Sundays after Pentecost, it breaks off after the Christmas material to provide the description of the Mass that is translated here. The description provides a somewhat simplified version of the elaborate papal Mass of *Ordo romanus I* and offers a brief and fairly clear picture of the Mass as it was celebrated outside Rome throughout much of the Middle Ages. Its occasionally cryptic language is illuminated by reference to the more detailed descriptions of the earlier *ordines romani* upon which it is based.

Ordo romanus XVII

17. The manner and order of performing the solemnities of the Mass on that very day [Christmas] and on all important festivals is to be as follows. The

TEXT: Michel Andrieu, ed., *Les Ordines romani du haut moyen âge,* vol. 3, Spicilegium sacrum Lovaniense, no. 28 (Louvain, 1961), pp. 178–83. Translation by James McKinnon.

priests and deacons, when the hour draws near for them to begin the Mass, enter the sacristy, clothe themselves with the proper vestments for Mass, and arrange themselves according to rank,[1] as is the custom.

18. And the clergy begins the antiphon[2] proper to that day.

19. When they commence the first verse of the psalm,[3] the priests leave the sacristy according to the date of their ordination, first those priests who are not celebrating the public Mass on that day, walking together two by two.

20. Then there follow those holding the candelabras with lighted tapers, both the seven and the two,[4] walking in pairs, and those with the tower-shaped censers, processing before the priest.

21. And the priest who will celebrate the Mass follows, with deacons to his left and to his right.

22. And other deacons follow these, walking in pairs. Similarly the subdeacons follow after them, proceeding rather slowly, moving with trembling and reverence.

23. When they come before the altar, they separate and face the space before the priest, looking across at each other.

24. The celebrant inclines his head in prayer and gives the peace to one priest on the right and to all his deacons. In doing this he faces in such a direction that, after demonstrating peace and harmony to the entire order of priests and his clergy, he might draw near to offer the sacrifice to God with a pure heart.

25. Then he approaches the altar and, with his entire body prostrate upon the floor, he pours out prayers for himself and for the sins of the people, until they sing the introit antiphon with the psalm and the *Gloria patri* with the verses *ad repentendum*.[5]

26. Arising from prayer he kisses the holy gospel book that is placed on the altar, he and all the deacons as well.

27. He moves behind the altar with his deacons and looks out from the East;[6] while the deacons remain next to him, one group on the right and the other on the left, the other priests stand next to the altar, arranged by their rank.

1. *Per ordines* and similar phrases are translated "according to rank" here, that is, presumably, according to the date of a cleric's ordination (see "according to the date of their ordination," *sicut sunt ordinati*) in paragraph 19 below.

2. "Antiphon," that is, the Introit antiphon.

3. "The psalm," that is, the Introit psalm; a complete psalm was still sung at this time with the Introit antiphon.

4. *Aut septem aut duo* is translated here "both the seven and the two"; the cryptic Latin phrase seems to distinguish between the seven candle holders that are typical in the entry processions of the *Ordines romani,* and the two that are to accompany the gospel procession (see paragraph 35 below).

5. To sing the verses *ad repentendum* is a Frankish practice by which one or more psalm verses are repeated after the *Gloria patri.*

6. The church is oriented, that is, the chancel is in the East end and the main entrance in the West; here the celebrant goes behind the altar and turns to face west, literally "from the East," toward the congregation and the west end.

28. When the Introit antiphon and the ninefold Kyrie eleison are completed, the priest, facing the people, begins the Gloria in excelsis Deo. And when they arrive at the words *pax hominibus bonae voluntatis* they look again toward the East[7] until the Gloria in excelsis Deo is completed.

29. Then the priest turns to the people and says, "Peace to you," and all respond, "And with your spirit."

30. Then he looks to the East and says the proper prayer of the day.

31. The celebrating priest then sits in his chair behind the altar, while the deacons remain standing at his side, and the other priests sit on benches next to the altar.

32. The lector now enters to read the Apostle.[8]

33. And the subdeacons go up around the altar so that they are ready for all that the deacons might require of them.

34. After the lesson is read, so too is the response.[9] sung and then the Alleluia.

35. The deacon then inclines his head toward the knees of the priest. After accepting the priest's blessing, the deacon proceeds to the altar, kisses the holy gospel book, and elevates it with his hands in great reverence. Going before him are two candelabras with lighted tapers, and the tower-shaped censer; he mounts the steps of the ambo, makes the sign of the cross on his forehead, looks up to heaven, and says, "The Lord be with you," and all respond, "And with your spirit." He then announces the gospel lesson and reads it.

36. When he has completed the reading, the priest says to him, "Peace to you." Next the priest says, "The Lord be with you," then, "Let us pray," and sits upon his chair.

37. Then an acolyte pours water on the hands of the priest, while the deacons dress the altar.

38. In a monastery where the people, including the women, are allowed to enter, the priest goes down from his chair with the deacons and accepts the offerings[10] from the people; he places these offerings in linen cloths which the acolyte is to carry before his breast.

39. Similarly the deacons accept the wine and place it in silver vessels, or chalices, which the acolytes are to carry.

40. After the reception of the offerings the priest returns to his chair and again washes his hands.

41. But in a monastery where women do not enter, after the first time the priest washes his hands, the priest and deacons go to the sacristy to receive the

---

7. The Latin has "from the East" (*ab oriente*), but it should be "to the east" (*ad orientem*); this is clear from the context, from the other *Ordines romani*, and from the universally-observed liturgical rubrics in this regard.

8. "The Apostle," referring to the Apostle Paul, is the standard early Christian and early medieval term for the epistle.

9. The "response" (*responsorium* here and *responsum* in certain other documents) is the contemporary term for the gradual.

10. That is, the bread.

gifts. They process then from the sacristy and the gifts are placed on the altar, while the brethren sing the offertory.

42. Then the priest goes to the altar and takes the proper offerings; he raises his eyes to heaven and his hands with the offerings, and prays to the Lord, then places the offerings on the altar.

43. Similarly he offers the wine.

44. The deacons go behind the priest and arrange themselves by rank, and the subdeacons go behind the altar and place themselves by rank, while the priests stand in order before the altar.

45. Then the celebrating priest, with the other priests on his right and left, offers a prayer.

46. He inclines his face to the earth and says the prayer in secret, with no one else able to hear it, until he arrives at the words: "through all ages of ages," and all reply, "Amen."

47. Immediately he says, "The Lord be with you," then, "Lift up your hearts," then, "Let us give thanks to the Lord our God," and then he commences the preface; he lifts his voice and proclaims the preface so that it may be heard by virtually all.

48. When he arrives at the words, "the dominations adore," all the priests and deacons incline their faces to the earth, and when he arrives at the words, "we sing in humble confession: *Sanctus*," the deacons bow again and the clergy with all the people.

49. As all proclaim the Sanctus with great reverence and trembling, the priest begins the canon,[11] in a contrastingly low voice.

50. The priests, deacons, and subdeacons remain bowed all the while up to the place where the priest says, "to us sinners also."

51. And when he arrives at the words, "deign to look upon us with a gracious and serence countenance," the priest inclines his head toward the altar and prays humbly until he says, "so that whatever from the participation in this sacrifice."

52. After the subdeacons arise, one of them goes and takes the paten from the acolyte and returns to where he stood in rank and holds the paten before his breast until the priest says, "all honor and glory."[12]

53. When the priest arrives at the words "through him and with him," he lifts the proper offerings from the altar and places them above the mouth of the chalice, which is held by the deacon who elevates it somewhat until the priest says, "through all ages of ages. Amen."

11. The canon (Latin for "rule") is the medieval term for the eucharistic prayer. Paragraphs 51–55 describe a series of inclinations and other actions that take place as the celebrating priest arrives at various points in the prayer. One notes that there is no elevation of host and chalice during the prayer; the elevation was not introduced until the early thirteenth century.

12. "All honor and glory" is the penultimate phrase of the canon; it is followed by "through all ages of ages. Amen." It is necessary to know this in order to follow the text of paragraphs 53–55, where the actions of the various ministers tend to overlap one another.

54. The priests and deacons remain continuously bowed in the same place except for the deacon who holds up the chalice.

55. The subdeacon who holds the paten gives it to the deacon at the point that the priest says, "all honor and glory." And the deacon holds it until the Lord's Prayer is finished and then hands it to the priest.

56. After the Lord's Prayer, the priest, while continuing to pray, takes the offerings and places them on the paten. He breaks off a small piece of the bread offering and places it in the chalice, makes the sign of the cross over it three times, and says: "The peace of the Lord be always with you."

57. And the people exchange the peace.

58. Then, if necessary, the priests first break up the bread offerings upon the altar, and then the deacons who are near the altar, as the subdeacon holds the paten before himself, break up these bread offerings [upon the paten], while the brethren sing *Agnus dei.*

59. Then the priests and the deacons receive communion according to their rank.

60. Afterwards the deacon takes the chalice to the right side of the altar, holding it up in his hands, and announces the festivals of the saints for the coming week in the following manner: "That approaching day is the feast of the holy Mary, or of a confessor, or of some other saint," whatever is to come according to the Martyrology.[13] And all respond: "Thanks be to God."

61. Then, after the singing of the communion antiphon, and the communion of all, the priest says the oration.

62. And the deacon sings, "Go the Mass is ended," and all reply, "Thanks be to God." And it is finished.

63. After this the priest returns to the sacristy with his ministers and all their paraphernalia, just as they previously exited from the sacristy. And they remove the vestments with which they celebrated the solemnities of the Mass. And now everything has been completed.

13. The Martyrology was a book, arranged by calendar, that listed the festivals of the martyrs and eventually other saints as well. It was used to announce the festivals of the coming week at a time when the clergy, let alone the laity, did not possess individual liturgical books.

12 Helisachar

The birth date of Helisachar, a Goth from the region of Septimania, is unknown. From 808 at latest he served in Aquitania as chancellor to Charlemagne's son Louis the Pious. After Louis became emperor in 814, Helisachar held the same post in the court at Aachen until about 817. He remained thereafter a figure of some importance in the court circle, working closely with Charlemagne's cousins Wala and Adalhard. Although a canon rather than a monk, who spent much of his career at court, he was appointed abbot of St. Aubin's of Angers and later of St. Riquier in Picardy, holding the latter position from 822 to 837.

Helisachar was an important figure in the Carolingian movement toward liturgical reform. He was probably the author of a preface and supplement to Alcuin's lectionary. The letter translated here, believed to have been written sometime between 819 and 822, describes his revision of an Office antiphonary.

Letter to Archbishop Nidibrius of Narbonne

I believe that your holy paternity recalls, when not long ago the command of the emperor bound me to service in his court at the palace in Aachen and held you there for the disposition of certain ecclesiastical affairs, that we often came together during the night hours for the celebration of the Divine Office, where the reading of holy scripture brought peace to our souls. But, as you frequently remarked, you were greatly troubled that the responsories were lacking in authority and reason,[1] and that the verses were inappropriately matched with certain of the responsories by both our cantors and yours.[2] You commissioned me, therefore, to explore the meadows of the sacred scriptures for appropriate verses, bringing to bear my experience and eagerness in compensation for my lack of native intelligence, and to match these verses suitably to responsories that have been authoritatively and rationally recorded. Granted that this task exceeds my powers, and that my ineptitude surpasses my ability to measure it; I could not presume, nevertheless, to neglect that which your holiness commands me to execute with absolute commitment. I placed my confidence in the gracious mercy of Him who has the power to satisfy your sacred wish through the agency of your weak and useless servant, and also to lend to my want of skill what is due to your merits and devotion.

Approaching this task, then, I first gathered from here and there antiphoners

---

TEXT: *Monumenta Germaniae Historica*, Epistolarum tomus V (Munich: MGH, 1978), pp. 307–309. Translation by James McKinnon.

1. Helisachar frequently uses the word authority (*auctoritas*) in this letter as a quality that liturgical chants ought to possess. In most cases the word seems to imply the authority derived from a biblical text, while at times it also seems to imply that such authority is conferred by the appearance of a chant in the majority of antiphoners.

2. One concludes from contemporary documents that the chief reason for this incongruity of verse and responsory is the result of the different manner of performing responsories at Rome and in Gaul. In Rome the entire response was repeated after the verse, but in Gaul only its latter portion, in most cases less than a complete sentence. This resulted, apparently, in numerous instances where there was a lack of coherence between the text of the verse and the text of the repeated portion of the response.

and cantors, and also an abundance of books and skilled readers, and then carefully set about to test the concordance of the antiphoners. Now, while they differed among themselves very little with respect to the chants of the Mass, which rest entirely upon the authority of the holy scriptures, few were found to manifest unity with respect to the chants of the Office,[3] even when these chants appear to have been derived from divine authority or from the writings of the Fathers. Some of the chants in these books were distorted by the error of scribes, some were removed at the whim of the unlearned, and some were jumbled together. It is altogether clear, then, that the antiphonary which was well edited with respect to the night offices by its author in the city of Rome, has been greatly corrupted by those who we mentioned above.

Although those who have the gift of understanding are able to choose that which should be approved and to reject that which should be disapproved, it was necessary, nonetheless, to obey your commands in every respect because of the simpleminded and the less intelligent. By means, therefore, of this persistent collecting and scrupulous examination of antiphoners, which revealed their numerous discrepancies, we have rejected those antiphons and responsories that were lacking in authority and reason and were thus unworthy to be sung in the praise of God. We have, moreover, assigned to their proper places those chants which are clearly authoritative, and we have to the best of our ability joined appropriate verses to them, calling upon that same authority which flows from the copious stream of books. Hence, as you have insisted yourself, a suitable verse is derived from the same source as was the responsory. There were actually some antiphons and responsories, altogether authoritative and suitable for the praise of God, which were unknown to both our cantors and yours. So I took care to call upon certain masters of the art of melody from whom our cantors and yours could eagerly learn these chants. Thus a sacred enterprise succeeds by dint of abundant grace, so that what has been justified by reason and authority is included in this work, and that what was lacking in these qualities is provided by the documentation of many books; and whatever was corrupted in various places by the negligence of scribes or the arrogance of cantors, or was omitted or added by the ignorant, is corrected by the zealous application of expertise and polished by the file of righteousness.

I humbly beg, then, that this project, carried out at your command and dedicated to your zeal, a work of singular necessity to our cantors and yours (even if not to others whom it may not please), be received favorably by you, my father, and be put to use with great devotion in the praise of God. Make available the work to those who will be content with it so that they may carefully copy it, but do not offer it to the fastidious and the ungrateful who are more inclined to criticize than to learn. And insist that those to whom it is lent will

3. Carolingian documents frequently refer to the Mass by the metonymy of "Gradual" (here *in gradali cantu*), and similar the Office by some form of the word "night" (here *in nocturnali* [*cantu*]). The latter usage stems from the circumstance that a large majority of the Office chants were sung at the night Office, commonly referred to today as Matins.

neither delete anything from it, nor add nor change anything, according to that adage of the blessed Jerome that there was nothing to be gained from the editing of books unless the emendation itself is preserved by the diligence of the scribes.

If there is anything in our work that can be faulted in any way (from a motive of arrogance rather than of humility), be assured that this is an instance of innocent dissimulation rather than something overlooked through carelessness or inexperience. For it was right that we approve by our silence, rather than presumptuously judge and tamper with, that which showed signs of wear from its long and devout use by many in the divine liturgy. Nothing of what your holiness finds arranged in this work, unless it be corrupted by subsequent neglect and carelessness, can be found guilty of improper admission to the praise of God; it was included either because it enjoyed scriptural authority, because it was composed from the sayings of the fathers, or because it was justified by the use of many in pious devotion over a long time.

Since we have deemed it appropriate to place this work before our cantors and yours, it is necessary that both the one group and the other take special care, since the verses have been properly placed and arranged, that they be sung accurately after the manner of the melodic art and that they be adapted at the right places in the responsories. It is necessary, moreover, that these chants—composed as they are according to the elegant standard of the melodic art and providing the cantors, as I have said, with a sterling example of something derived from that art—are well understood so that, by the careful observation of all this, there will be no straying in any way from the authority of the melodic art.

May the holy triune God keep you continually mindful of me in his holy service, my father, you who are to be venerated with honor and honored with veneration.

13 John the Deacon

John the Deacon, surnamed Hymonides, was probably a monk of Monte Cassino in the mid-eighth century. He resided for a while in the Frankish court of Charles the Bald (d. 877), and then returned to Italy, where he served in the administration of Pope John VIII (872–882). He died sometime before 882.

His biography of Gregory the Great, commissioned by John VIII, is a highly partisan work, glorifying both Gregory and Rome. Some of the details of the musical portion of the biography, translated here, are strikingly similar to those encountered in the reading from the Monk of St. Gall (even if their interpretation varies sharply). Perhaps both authors heard the same stories from members of the Frankish court.

FROM *Life of Gregory the Great*

6. Then, in the house of the Lord, after the manner of the most wise Solomon, the exceedingly diligent Gregory, motivated by the compunction[1] of musical sweetness, compiled a centonate antiphoner of chants,[2] a task of great usefulness. He also founded the *schola cantorum*, which still sings in the holy church of Rome according to its original instructions. And he built two dwellings for the *schola*, with the proceeds from some plots of land: one near the steps of the basilica of St. Peter the Apostle, and another near the lodgings of the Lateran palace,[3] where even today are preserved with fitting reverence, the bed on which Gregory lay while singing, the switch with which he threatened the boys, as well as the authentic antiphoner. He subdivided these dwellings through a series of injunctions subject to the penalty of anathema for the sake of the daily convenience of the ministry at both places.[4]

7. Of the various European peoples it was the Germans and the Gauls who were especially able to learn and repeatedly to relearn the suavity of the schola's song, but they were by no means able to maintain it without distortion, as much because of their carelessness (for they mixed in with the Gregorian chants some of their own) as because of their native brutishness. For Alpine bodies, which make an incredible din with the thundering of their voices, do not properly echo the elegance of the received melody, because the barbaric savagery of a drunken gullet, when it attempts to sing the gentle cantilena with its inflections and repercussions, emits, by a kind of innate cracking, rough tones with a confused sound like a cart upon steps. And so it disquiets the

TEXT: Jacques Migne, ed., *Patrologia cursus completus. Series latina*, vol. 75 (Paris, 1884), cols. 90–92. Translation by James McKinnon.

1. Compunction *(compunctio)*, a highly favored word among medieval religious authors, connotes a sort of sweetly sorrowful remorse for one's sins.
2. "A centonae antiphoner of chants" *(antiphonarium centonem cantorum)*, a difficult and perhaps corrupt phrase; *centonem*, a substantive rather than adjective form, means, literally, something sewn together from patches.
3. The text has the dwelling at St. Peter's located *sub gradibus* and that at the Lateran, *sub domibus*. *Sub* can mean either "below" or "near"; "near," the more inclusive of the two meanings, is chosen here as a matter of caution. The steps at St. Peter's that John had in mind are most probably the prominent stairway that led from the great atrium at the east of the basilica to the plaza below.
4. This somewhat awkward sentence (what could be the meaning of subdividing dwellings through a series of injunctions?) has received little notice in the musicological literature. It is very significant in its suggestion that the *schola cantorum* sang both for papal ceremonies at the Lateran and for urban ceremonies at the basilica of St. Peter's, thus casting strong doubt on theories that there were separate papal and urban chant dialects in early medieval Rome.

spirits of those listeners that it should have mollified, irritating and disturbing them instead.

8. Hence it is that in the time of this Gregory, when Augustine went to Britain, cantors of the Roman school were dispersed throughout the West and instructed the barbarians with distinction. After they died the Western churches so corrupted the received body of chant that a certain John, a Roman cantor (together with Theodore, a Roman citizen yet also archbishop of York), was sent by bishop Vitalian[5] to Britain by way of Gaul; and John recalled the children of the churches in every place to the pristine sweetness of the chant, and preserved for many years, as much by himself as through his disciples, the rule of Roman doctrine.

9. But our patrician Charles,[6] the king of the Franks, disturbed when at Rome by the discrepancy between the Roman and the Gallican chant, is said to have asked—when the impudence of the Gauls argued that the chant was corrupted by certain tunes of ours, while on the contrary our melodies demonstrably represented the authentic antiphoner—whether the stream or the fountain is liable to preserve the clearer water. When they replied that it was the fountain, he wisely added: "Therefore it is necessary that we, who have up to now drunk the tainted water of the stream, return to the flowing source of the perennial fountain." Shortly afterward, then, he left two of his diligent clergymen with Hadrian, a bishop at the time, and, after they had been schooled with the necessary refinement, he employed them to recall the province of Metz to the sweetness of the original chant, and through her, to correct his entire region of Gaul.

10. But when after a considerable time, with those who had been educated at Rome now dead, that most sage of kings had observed that the chant of the other Gallican churches differed from that of Metz, and had heard someone boasting that one chant had been corrupted by the other; "Again," he said, "let us return to the source." Then Pope Hadrian, moved by the pleas of the king (as some today reliably confirm), sent two cantors to Gaul, by whose counsel the king recognized that all indeed had corrupted the suavity of the Roman chant by a sort of carelessness, and saw that Metz, in fact, differed by just a little, and only because of native savagery. Finally, even today, it is confirmed by those who love the simple truth, that as much as the chant of Metz cedes to the Roman, so much does the chant of the other Gallican and German churches cede to the church of Metz. I have mentioned all this by way of anticipation, lest I seem to pass over in silence the carelessness of the Gauls.

5. Theodore was in fact sent to Britain by Pope Vitalian (657–672) in 668, but John was sent a decade later, 678, by Pope Agatho (678–681).

6. Both Charles, and his father Pepin, were formally invested with the title "patrician of the Romans" by contemporary popes.

14 The Monk of St. Gall

A monk from the abbey of St. Gall composed a life of Charlemagne in about 884. At one point in the work he described himself as "toothless and stammering," a remark that suggests he might well be identified with Notker Balbulus ("Notker the stammerer"), a monk of St. Gall who lived from about 840 to 912.

The life is less a proper biography than a collection of anecdotes, many of them quite fanciful. The anecdotes are organized into an opening series on Charlemagne's "piety and his care for the Church" and a second series on his military exploits; a contemplated third series on his daily life was never written. Some see the story translated here as a direct reply to John the Deacon's unflattering remarks about Frankish chanting, but a comparison of the texts fails to establish such a connection between them. More likely, perhaps, is that both rely on the same source.

FROM *Life of the Emperor Charles the Great*

BOOK I

10. At this point I must relate a story that the men of our time might find difficult to believe, since even I who write it would still not entirely believe it—because of the great dissimilarity between our chant and that of the Romans—were it not that the veracity of the fathers is more credible than the flippant deceitfulness of the present generation. Charles, that tireless devotee of the divine liturgy, glad that his vow to do everything that he could for the discipline of letters had been fulfilled, yet sad that all the provinces, regions, and cities differed from one another in the divine praises, that is, in the melodies of the chant, took care to request from Stephen, pope of blessed memory, that he send additional clerics who were greatly skilled in the divine chant. It was Stephen who, after that wretched king of the Franks Childeric was deposed and had his head shorn, annointed Charles to the helm of kingship after the manner of the ancient fathers.[1] Stephen, benevolently disposed and

TEXT: Hans Haefele, ed. *Gesta Karoli Magni Imperatoris*, Monumenta Germaniae Historica, Scriptores rerum germanicarum, n.s., vol. 12 (Berlin: MGH, 1959), pp. 12–15. Translation by James McKinnon.

1. Pope Stephen II (752–757) annointed not Charles, but his father Pepin III, who reigned from 751 to his death in 768. Pepin, with the blessing of Pope Zacharias (741–752), deposed Childeric III in 751 and had him confined to a monastery.

inspired by his sacred studies as well,[2] gave assent and dispatched from the Apostolic See to Charles in Francia twelve clerics who were greatly learned in the chant, according to the number of the twelve apostles.

By Francia, incidentally, which I have just mentioned, I mean all the provinces beyond the Alps. For just as it is written, "In those days ten men from all the tongues of the nations shall hold fast the shirt of a man who is a Jew,"[3] at that time, because of the eminence of the glorious Charles, the Gauls and Aquitanians, the Aedui and Spaniards, the Germans and Bavarians, all prided themselves as greatly complemented if they merited to be called servants of the Franks.

When the above-mentioned clerics departed from Rome, they plotted among themselves (since all Greeks and Romans are ever consumed with envy of Frankish glory) how they could so alter the chant that its unity and harmony might never be enjoyed in a realm and province other than their own. So they came to Charles and were received with honor and dispersed to the most prestigious locations. And, in these various localities, everyone of them strove to sing, and to teach others to sing, as differently and as corruptly as they could possibly contrive. But the exceedingly clever Charles celebrated the feasts of Christmas and the Epiphany one year at Trier and Metz and very alertly and sharply comprehended the quality of the chants, indeed penetrated to their very essence, and then in the next year he followed the same festivals at Paris and Tours and heard nothing of that sound which he had experienced the year before in the above-mentioned places. Thus he discovered in the course of time how those he had sent to different places had come to differ from one another, and he conveyed the matter to Pope Leo of blessed memory, the successor to Stephen.[4] Leo, after recalling the cantors to Rome and condemning them to exile or to lifelong confinement, said to the illustrious Charles: "If I send others to you, they, blinded by envy like those before them, will not neglect to deceive you. Rather I will attempt to satisfy your wishes in this manner: give me two very intelligent clerics of your own, in such a way as not to alert my clergy that they belong to you, and they shall acquire, God willing, the total proficiency in this skill that you seek."

It was done in this way, and after a reasonable length of time Leo returned the clerics to Charles perfectly instructed. Charles kept one with himself, and sent the other, at the request of his son Drogo, bishop of Metz, to that church. The second cleric's industry not only held sway in that place, but came to be spread through all of Francia, to such an extent that now even among the

---

2. "Inspired by his sacred studies," more literally, "by his divinely inspired studies"; this appears to refer to a somewhat feeble instance of allegorical exegesis—the studious Stephen, inspired by reading of the scriptural twelve apostles, sends the same number of cantors from the Apostolic See.

3. Zacharias 8:23.

4. Leo, presumably Leo III (795–816), was not the immediate successor to Stephen; thirty-eight years and several popes intervened between their reigns.

people in those regions where they speak Latin, the ecclesiastical song is called the *mettensis*. Among us, however, who speak the Teutonic or Germanic language, it is called in the vernacular *met* or *mette,* or to use the word of Greek derivation, *mettisca.* Charles, moreover, the most benign emperor, sent the cantor who had been assigned to him, Peter by name, to stay for a while at the monastery of St. Gall; and since Charles was the powerful patron of St. Gall, he made the choir a gift of an authentic antiphoner and he took care that they be instructed so that they learned to sing in the Roman manner, as they do today.

15 Hildegard of Bingen

Hildegard was born in 1098 to noble parents near Spanheim in the Rhineland. She was dedicated to the Church from infancy and took the veil as a girl of fifteen at the Benedictine cloister of Disiboden, where she became superior in 1136. In about 1150 she founded her own convent on the Rupertsberg, in the Rhine Valley near Bingen. She remained there until her death in 1179, attracting a wide following through the fame of her prophetic visions. Known as the "Sibyl of the Rhine," her advice was sought by no less than popes, bishops, and kings. She was a person of extraordinarily varied talents; the author of mystical works, medical works, liturgical poetry set to music, and a morality play.

The excerpt translated here is from a letter she wrote near the end of her life to the hierarchy of Mainz. They had ordered—as punishment for Hildegard's alleged burying of an excommunicated individual in the consecrated ground of her convent's cemetery—that the nuns of the convent be deprived of the sacraments and that they be forbidden to celebrate the Office with music. Hildegard's letter, which recounts what she saw and heard in a vision, reveals at once the pain of being deprived of the sung Office, and her view of music's profoundly spiritual nature.

FROM *Epistle 47: To the Prelates of Mainz*

And I saw something beyond this—as in obedience to you we have until now given up the singing of the Divine Office, celebrating it only by quiet reading— and I heard a voice coming from the living light, telling of those various kinds of praise concerning which David speaks in the Psalms: "Praise him with the

TEXT: *Patrologia Latina* 197, cols. 219–21. Translation by James McKinnon.

sound of the trumpet, praise him with the psaltery and the cithara, praise him with the tympanum and the chorus, praise him with strings and the organ, praise him with the well-sounding cymbals, praise him with the cymbals of jubilation. Let every spirit praise the Lord."[1] In these words we are taught about inward concerns by external objects, how according to the makeup of material things (the properties of musical instruments) we ought best to convert and to refashion the workings of our interior man to the praise of the Creator. When we earnestly strive so to praise, we recall how man sought the voice of the living Spirit, which Adam lost through disobedience, he, who still innocent before his transgression, had no little concourse with the voices of angelic praise (which angels, who are always called spirits, thanks to the Spirit who is God, possess by reason of their spiritual nature). Thus Adam lost that likeness of an angelic voice which he had in Paradise, and thus he went to sleep in that musical science with which he was endowed before his sin. And upon awakening from his slumber he was rendered unaware and uncertain of what he had witnessed in his dreams, when deceived by a prompting from the Devil, and repudiating the will of his Creator, he became entangled in the darkness of inner ignorance because of his sin. But God, who restores the souls of the elect to their original state of bliss by the light of truth, wrought this in his wisdom: that when the Spirit renewed, with a prophetic infusion, the heart of however many, they recovered, by reason of this interior illumination, whatever had been lost from that which Adam possessed before the punishment for his derilection of duty.

But so that mankind, rather than recall Adam in his exile, be awakened to those things also—the divine sweetness and the praise which Adam had enjoyed before his fall—the same holy prophets, taught by that Spirit which they had received, not only composed psalms and canticles, which were to be sung in order to kindle the devotion of those hearing them, but also invented diverse instruments of the musical art, which would be played with a great variety of sound. They did so for this reason: so that the listeners would—as much from the construction and sound of these instruments, as from the meaning of the words sung to their accompaniment—be educated in interior matters, as said above, while being urged on and prodded by exterior objects. Wise and studious men imitated these holy prophets and invented numerous types of human instruments, so that they could make music for the delight of their souls, and adapt what they sang by the bending of their finger joints, as if recalling Adam who was formed by the finger of God (who is the Holy Spirit)— that Adam in whose voice, before he fell, resided the sound of all harmony and the sweetness of the entire musical art, and the power and sonority of whose voice (had he remained in that state in which he was created) the fragility of mortal men could not sustain.

1. Psalm 150.3–6.

But when his deceiver, the Devil, heard what man had begun to sing by the inspiration of God, and that man was invited by this to recall the sweetness of the songs of heaven, seeing that his cunning machinations had gone awry, he was so frightened that he was greatly tormented, and he continually busied himself in scheming and in selecting from the multifarious falsehoods of his iniquity, so that he did not cease to disrupt that affirmation and beauty of divine praise and spiritual hymnody, withdrawing it not only from the heart of man by evil suggestions, unclean thoughts, and various distractions, but even (wherever possible) from the heart of the Church, through dissension, scandal, and unjust oppression. Wherefore you and all other prelates must exercise the greatest care, and before you silence by your decrees the voice of some congregation that sings the praises of God, or before you suspend it from administering or receiving the sacraments, you must first air the reasons for doing this by the most meticulous investigation.

And pay heed that you are led to take such action by zeal for the justice of God, rather than by anger, by some unjust impulse, or by the desire for revenge, and always beware of being circumvented in your judgments by Satan, who deprived man of celestial harmony and the delights of Paradise. And consider, that just as the body of Jesus Christ was born of the Holy Spirit from the purity of the Virgin Mary, so too was the song of praise born in the Church according to celestial harmony through the Holy Spirit; for the body is in truth the clothing of the soul, which has a living voice, and thus it is fitting that the body, together with the soul, sing praises to God through its own voice. Whence the Prophetic Spirit proclaims symbolically[2] that God is to be praised on cymbals of jubilation and on other musical instruments, which clever and industrious men invented, since all the arts that contribute to the utility and need of mankind were discovered by some breath that God sent into the body of man.[3] Thus it is just that God be praised in everything. And since man sighs and moans with considerable frequency upon hearing some song, as he recalls in his soul the quality of celestial harmony, the prophet David, considering with understanding the nature of what is spiritual (because the soul is harmonious) exhorts us in the psalm, "Let us confess the Lord on the cithara, let us play to him on the psaltery of ten strings,"[4] intending that the cithara, which sounds from below, pertains to the discipline of the body; that the psaltery, which sounds from above, pertains to the striving of the spirit; and that the ten strings

2. *Per significationem* is translated "symbolically" here; this is an obvious reference to the standard allegorical treatment of musical instruments referred to above in note 3 of the reading from St. Basil (pp. 12–13) and note 6 of the reading from St. John Chrysostom (p. 16). In most circumstances such symbolic reference to musical instruments implies that actual musical instruments were not in use. However, by dwelling on the subject in the present reading, Hildegard creates the impression that the playing of instruments in her convent might very well have been a common practice, now forbidden by the Mainz hierarchy.

3. Compare Genesis 2.7.

4. Psalm 32(33).1.

refer to the contemplation of the Law.[5] Thus they who without the weight of sure reason impose silence upon a church in the matter of songs in praise of God, and thereby unjustly deprive God of the honor of his praise on earth, will be deprived themselves of the participation in the angelic praises heard in Heaven, unless they make amends by true regret and humble penitence.

5. There are three instances here of that symbolical treatment of biblical instruments referred to above in note 2; each of them is met with again and again in the exegetical literature of the patristic and medieval periods. The cithara (a type of lyre, with its sounding chamber at the bottom of the instrument) was taken to refer to the more mundane virtues, such as self-denial; the psaltery (probably understood by the Church Fathers as a triangular harp with its sounding chamber on its upper member) was taken to refer to the more spiritual virtues such as the practice of contemplation; while the ten strings of the psaltery were taken to refer to the Ten Commandments.

Music Theory and Pedagogy in the Middle Ages

16 Anonymous (9th Century)

The *Musica enchiriadis,* along with the *Scolica enchiriadis,* a short dialogue of related character that appears with it in most manuscripts, is of uncertain date and provenance. It is generally assumed to have been written toward the end of the ninth century somewhere in the north of the Carolingian realm. It has long been celebrated as the earliest surviving witness to Western polyphonic music, but the central focus of the treatise is on describing a tonal matrix for Gregorian chant. It shares this profoundly significant task with Huchbald's *De harmonica institutione* (translated in Claude Palisca, ed., *Hucbald, Guido, and John on Music* [New Haven: Yale University Press, 1978], 13–46), of slightly earlier date perhaps, and the anonymous *Alia musica,* thought to be compiled somewhat later.

At the core of the *Musica's* tonal system is a tetrachord corresponding to the modern notes D, E, F, and G, the four finals of the ecclesiastical modes. The tetrachord is repeated at various pitch levels to create a gamut that has scandalized some modern observers with its augmented octaves, but which matches the tonality of Gregorian chant better than the Boethian scale. It is expressed in a precise and ingenious—if rather ungainly—system of notation called daseian, from its use of the Greek aspirant (the *prosodia daseia,* ⊣.)

FROM THE *Musica enchiriadis*

I. Beginning of the Handbook on Music

Just as letters are the elementary and indivisable parts of articulated speech, from which syllables and in turn verbs and nouns are formed to create the text of finished discourse, so too the pitches *(ptongi)*[1] of sung speech, which the Latins call sounds *(soni),* are themselves basic elements, and the totality of music is encompassed in their ultimate realization. From the combination of these sounds intervals are created, and from the intervals, in turn, scales *(systemata);* sounds are in truth the primary material of song. Pitches, however, are not just any kind of sound, but those which are suitable to melody by legitimate spacing between themselves. They have a certain natural order in their rise and fall so that a similarly constituted group of four pitches[2] appears

TEXT: Hans Schmid, ed., *Musica et scolica enchiriadis* (Munich: C. H. Beck, 1981), pp. 3–20. Translation by James McKinnon. (The entire treatise is translated by Raymond Erickson, *Musica enchiriadis and Scolica enchiriadis* [New Haven: Yale University Press, 1995].)

1. It would be comforting to the translator of medieval theory if there were unambiguous English equivalents to the Greek and Latin terms for musical pitches, but there are not. There is an attempt here to maintain consistency in translating *ptongus* as "pitch," *sonus* as "sound", and *nota* as "note" (the author of the *Musica enchiriadis* in fact offers definitions for the first two of these later in the paragraph). However, consistency of translation is not always possible, and there are passages later in this reading where it seems advisable to translate *sonus* as "note."
2. That is, a tetrachord.

four times in succession. But all four tetrachords, while dissimilar, are so internally homogeneous, that not only do they differ by height and depth, but it is in this very height and depth that they have the distinct quality of their nature, which is provided by a legitimate distance upwards or downward from each other.[3] To provide an example now, these are the notes *(notae)* of the tetrachord in their proper order:

t	ꜰ	The first and lowest, called *protos* or *archoos* by the Greeks;
	ꞁ	The second or *deuterus,* separated from the protus by a tone;
s	ꜰ	The third or *tritus,* separated from the deuterus by a semitone;
t	ꜰ	The fourth or *tetrardus,* separated from the tritus by a tone.

An unending succession of these sounds is created by their multiplication; it continues throughout the four tetrachords of similar make-up until they run out either by ascending or descending.

To illustrate:

As this little diagram shows, whether you trace the sounds in upward or downward order until the last note, the series of tetrachords of this sort does not cease. The quality of these four sounds, moreover, creates the power of the eight modes, as will be described later in the proper place. The complete agreement of these tetrachords is achieved by a sort of amiable diversity.

While, as has been said, their repetition leads to an immeasurable quantity, the logic of our discipline extracts a set number from this confusing multitude, confining its investigation to eighteen sounds. The first and lowest among them consists in the tetrachord of the *graves;* next to it comes the tetrachord of the *finales.* After these come the tetrachord of the *superiores,* and then of the *excellentes.* There remain two final sounds. A diagram of all this follows:

II. THE SYMBOLS OF THE PITCHES AND WHY THERE ARE EIGHTEEN

Since, as we have said, nature has decreed that there are four sets of four similarly related notes, so too are their symbols nearly identical. The difference between the tetrachords is indicated only by the various reversals of the characters.

---

3. This highly abstract sentence appears only to make the simple point that since each of the four tetrachords has the same configuration of half and whole steps, the four differ only by their higher or lower placement in the gamut.

The first final or end-note [D] has an inclined daseian F

with S at its top, thus *Ϝ*

The second final [E] has a reversed C on top,   thus *Ϥ*
The third final [F] has a simple inclined I or *iota*,   thus *I*
The fourth final [G] has a half-C on top,   thus *Ϝ*
The *graves* reverse the finals,   thus *ꟿ ꟿ N ꟿ*
The *superiores* invert the finals,   thus *ꟿ ꟿ ꟿ ꟿ*
The *excellentes* invert the *graves*,   thus *Ƚ Ƚ Ƚ Ƚ*

The third note is an exception to this: in the *graves* it has an inclined N *N*; in the *superiores* a reversed and inclined N *Ͷ*; and in the *excellentes* a transfixed iota *Ŧ*. The two remaining signs have the recumbent forms of the protus and deuterus ⌐ᴎ ⌐ᴧ. There are eighteen notes all told, allowing each of them to achieve its largest consonance, that is, the fifteenth, about which more later.[4] There were many other signs created in antiquity for other sounds, but it behooves us to begin with what is easier.

III. WHY THE FINALS ARE NAMED AS SUCH

The finals or end-notes *(terminales soni)* are so called because it is necessary that every melody end on one of them. Melodies of the first mode and of its plagal *(subjugalis)* are ruled by and conclude on the low sound of the tetra-chord *Ϝ*. The second mode and its plagal is ruled by and concludes on the second sound *Ϥ*. The third mode and its plagal is ruled by and concludes on the third sound *I*. The fourth mode and its plagal is ruled by and concludes on the fourth sound *Ϝ*. The greater mode is called the authentic, the lesser, the plagal.

IV. WHY THERE IS ONLY ONE TETRACHORD BELOW THE FINALS BUT TWO ABOVE

The finals or end-notes have one tetrachord beneath them, called *graves*, but two above, the *superiores* and *excellentes* along with the two supernumer-ary notes. This is so because a natural and legitimate chant does not descend lower than the fifth sound below its final: to be more specific, this distance in the first and second modes is from low *Ϝ* [D] or the protus final to the corres-ponding note of the graves *ꟿ* [G]; in the third and fourth modes it is from the deuterus final *Ϥ* [E] to the corresponding note in the graves *ꟿ* [A]; in the fifth and sixth modes from the tritus final *I* [F] to the corresponding note in the graves *N* [B]; and in the seventh and eighth modes from the tetrardus final *Ϝ* [G] to the corresponding note in the graves *ꟿ* [C]. On the other hand, a chant may ascend from a given final to the third sound of the same name, that is, into the excellentes.[5]

4. Whatever the precise intention of this statement, it is clear that not every note can have its fifteenth or double-octave within an eighteen-note system.
5. Thus it may ascend two tetrachords (to the "third" if one counts the tetrachord of the finals itself), or a ninth, above the final.

V. How the Authentic and Plagal Modes Differ

Since an authentic mode and the plagal beneath it are governed by and conclude on the same note, they are considered to be one mode; yet they differ in that the plagal *(minores)* modes ascend by lesser *(minora)* intervals, with a particular plagal mode going no higher than the fifth sound over its final, and even this is rare.

VI. On the Characteristics of the Notes and How Many Steps Separate Notes of the Same Character

Whoever finds pleasure in studying these questions should take care to distinguish the peculiar properties of an individual sound, and then immediately to grasp its pitch within a group of notes, relative to what is below it or above, so as clearly to see, by both its nature and its notational symbol, how far it is distant from a related note. Every musical note has at the fifth step in either direction a note of the same character, and at the third step on either side of it there is a similar note as well;[6] while the note that is a second away on this side or that, will be a fourth away on the other. To those little practiced in these pursuits, something more should be provided, something by which they can learn to detect the peculiar properties of the notes in any familiar melody and also to explore an unknown melody by the quality and order of the notes as revealed by the notational symbols. It is of no small benefit to this enquiry if the Greek names of the individual pitches are sung through the neighboring notes in order, as follows:

[DFED]	[ECDE]	[FEF]	[GbG]
ΓΙ ΓΓ	*ΓꝬ ΓΓ*	*Ι ΓΙ*	*ΓꝬ Γ*
protus	deuterus	tritus	tetrardus[7]

VII. A Little Illustration of the Properties of The Notes for the Sake of Practice

Thus if any note is sung with its own name, one easily recognizes both the note and its name in the act of singing. By way of an example there follows a diagrammed song; it is sung by the musical symbols inscribed over each syllable, while the names of the notes are given above them in this way:

6. The notes a third step on either side are related to each other (they occupy the same position in their respective tetrachord), not to the central note.

7. This appears to be a kind of solmization, although one wonders about its practicality if the daseian symbols have to be translated into some sort of (presumably awkward) verbal code. (In reproducing this illustration, I have taken the liberty of choosing only four of six given examples, and of reordering these.)

Se	𝄢	tetrardos	Te	𝄢	tetrardos	Ty	𝄢	tetrardos	Rex	𝄢	tetrardos
ni		tetrardos	hu		tetrardos	ta		archoos	cae		archoos
be		archoos	mi.		archoos	nis·		deuteros	li:		deuteros
as		deuteros	les		deuteros	n.		tritos	do		tritos
fla		tritos	fa		tritos	ti.		tetrardos	mi.		tetrardos
gi.		tritos	mu		tritos	fi:		tetrardos	ne		tetrardos
tant		deuteros	hi:		deuteros						
va		tetrardos	bo		tetrardos						
ri.		deuteros	du		deuteros	ma		archoos	squa		archoos
is·		archoos	lis·		archoos	ris·		archoos	li:		archoos
hi:		tetrardos	ve		tetrardos	un		tetrardos	fi:		tetrardos
be		archoos	ne		archoos	fi:		tritos	que		tritos
ra		tetrardos	ran		tetrardos	so		archoos	so		archoos
re		tritos	do		tritos	n.		deuteros	li:		deuteros
ma		archoos	pi.		archoos						
lis:		deuteros	is·		deuteros						

But should there remain doubt about the pitch of any note, then one works through the notes in succession—guided by the placement of the semitones, which always separate the second and third note of a tetrachord—and it will quickly be revealed. This practice will make it possible to record and sing sounds no less easily than to copy and read letters. However all this has been phrased, it is intended to aid novices in their studies.

VIII. How All the Modes Are Derived from the Tetrachord

It must now be shown how the force of this tetrachord defines the modes (which we improperly call tones); the illustration will be arranged as follows. A series of quasi strings is set out in order with the notational symbols placed at their edge; the strings represent the pitches which the characters signify.

Between the strings a segment of some chant *(neuma)* is inserted, like this for example:

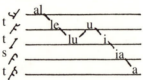

And now, in order to corroborate what has been said by both sight and sound, there follows another little diagram using the same *neuma*. After the strings have again been drawn from side to side, the *neuma* is inscribed within the strings in a fourfold series, with each of the four distinguished by its own color.[8] The first series begins at the note ↙ [A] and ends on the note ♭ [D]. The second starts at the note ↗ [B] and concludes on the note ♭ [E]. The third commences on the note ↰ [c] and leaves off at the note *I* [F]. The fourth arises from the note ↗ [d] and comes to a halt on the note *Ƒ* [G]. Thus:

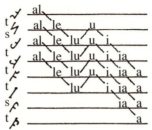

These four short examples, while separated from each other by only a tone or semitone (that is one step of the scale),[9] are transformed by that single step alone from one genus to another. When you sing the first series you can discern that the force of the first note ♭ [D] creates the character of the first mode, what we call protus authentic. When you sing the second, you hear that the deuterus mode is governed by the second note ♭ [E]. To take the third, you see again that the power of the tritus mode resides in the third note *I* [F]. And after you have sung the fourth, you will understand that the genus of the tetradus mode derives from the fourth note *Ƒ* [G].

Thus any melody of the first mode and its plagal can be treated like the first chant in the example below: and second mode melodies like the second, and third like the third, and fourth like the fourth. I have endeavored to make this especially clear by producing the examples in a dual format: by the precise placement of each notational symbol within the text, and graphically by the use of quasi strings.

8. One wonders if some manuscripts will exploit this opportunity to display attractive coloring.
9. The Latin has, "by an *armonico spacio*"; this refers, apparently, to the ancient science of harmonics, which concerns itself with the pitch relationships among the tones of the musical systems or scales. In the simplified medieval understanding of these systems, tones and semitones are the basic currency, whereas the ancients admitted a great variety of microtones.

A melody of the first mode and its plagal:

Al✔le✔lu /F/ ia ↗↘ . Lau✔da ↗✔ te✔ Do↗mi✔num✔ de /F cae ↗ lis ↗ .

		a							
	da	te	num						
Lau		mi	de		Cae	lo		e	
	Do		e		li	rum		te	
			caelis.		cae	lau	da	Deum.	
						au			

Cae /li ↗ cae ↗lo /rum ✔ lau ↗↗ da ↗te ✔/ De ↗ um ↗.

A melody of the second mode and its plagal:

Al ✔le ✔lu ↗✔↗ ia /F .
Con↗fi ✔te ↗ bor ✔F Do✔mi✔no ✔ ni ✔mis ✔ in ✔ o F/ re ↗ me ↗o ↗.

	te								
	fi	bo	ni						
		Domi	mis				e		
Con	r	no	in o		Lauda		me um	vita	
			o		a	um	in	a	
			meo.		De			mea.	
			re		bo				

Lau ↗da ↗ bo ↗ De ↗um /me ↗✔ um ✔ in /vi ↗ta ↗/ me ↗a ↗.

A melody of the third mode and its plagal:

Al ↗ le ✔ lu ✔✔✔ ia ↗/.
In ↗ tel ↗ le ↗✔ ge ✔ cla✔mo✔rem✔ me✔um✔ Do✔mi↗ne/.

Intelle							
	e						
	ge clamorem me	Do		re	e		
		um	mi	se	re	me i	
			ne.	Mi	e	Deus.	

Mi /se ↗ re ✔re ↗/ me ↗✔ i ↗ De /us/.

A melody of the fourth mode and its plagal:

Al ✔le ↗lu ✔↗✔ ia ✔↗.
Sit ✔✔ no ✔men ↗ Do ✔ mi ✔ni ↗ be ↗✔ ne ✔dic ✔↗ tum ✔ in ✔ sae ↗cu ↗la ↗.

		o						
Siit		Do mi						
	men	ni be	c		In	ter		
	no		e di		ae		e	
			ne	tum in		num	sae culum sae	
				saecula.		e in		e uli.
						t		cu

In ↗ ae ✔ter ↗ num ✔e ↗t/ in ↗ sae ✔✔cu ✔lum ✔ sae ✔↗cu /↗li ↗.

In the same way, in order to explore the nature of each mode, we use the customary melodic formulas composed according to the corresponding principles. The authentic melodic formulas begin in the superiores and conclude on the finals; while the plagal formulas begin in the area of the finals and remain there, without reaching that of the superiores. This is the case with NOAN-NOEANE, NOEAGIS, etc. which we believe are not so much words with meaning as syllables assigned to a melodic formula.

17 Anonymous (10th Century)

The *Alia musica* is a compilation, completed probably in the earlier tenth century, from the work of at least three different theorists; indeed the word *alia* in its title may be a Latin transliteration of *halia,* the Greek word for compilation (see p. 19 of the Heard dissertation cited in the Text note below). The composite nature of the treatise has given rise to differences of opinion over the proper order of its material and over which of the anonymous theorists saw to its final form (the principal protagonists in this controversy are Heard and Jacques Chailley [see citation in the Text note below]).

Whatever the ultimate answer to such questions, the treatise adds up to a thorough treatment of the ecclesiastical modes, emphasizing in particular the arithmetical proportions underlying their tonal makeup. The section of it translated here is of special interest for two reasons: its introduction of the concept of octave species into medieval modal theory and its assignment of the classical Greek modal names to the medieval modes, establishing them permanently in spite of their obvious incongruity.

FROM THE *Alia musica*

Let us, now that these matters have been attended to, proceed to the system of eight tropes, which the Latins call modes. First off it should be known that a trope, taken over from Greek into Latin, is said to be a *conversio* because something is converted into something else, except for that which is proper to it. Tones are referred to as such because they are, except for semitones, the

TEXT: Edmund Heard, "'Alia Musica': A Chapter in the History of Medieval Music Theory" (Ph.D. diss., University of Wisconsin, 1966), 125–31. Translation by James McKinnon. See also Jacques Chailley, *Alia musica (Traité de musique du IXème siècle)* (Paris: Centre de Documentation Universitaire, 1965), 105–110.

unique common currency of all the tropes. Modes also are referred to as such because each of the tropes must maintain its individual character *(modus)* and not exceed its proper measure *(mensura)*.[1]

Once a system has been established—one that is woven together from the duple, triple, quadruple, sesquialtera, and sesquitertial proportions,[2] with the notes of the fifteen strings interspersed[3]—it becomes necessary to name the eight tropes or modes.

The first mode, the lowest of all, will be called the Hypodorian; it uses the first species of octave and terminates on the middle string, called the mese [a].[4] The second mode is the Hypophrygian; it forms the second species of octave and terminates on the paramese [b]. The third mode is the Hypolydian, consisting in the third species of octave and ending on the string they call the trite diezeugmenon [c]. The fourth mode, the Dorian, reproduces the fourth species of octave and ends on the paranete diezeugmenon [d]. The fifth mode, the Phrygian, is confined to the fifth species of octave; its last string is the nete diezeugmenon [e]. The sixth mode, or Lydian, inescapably utilizes the sixth species of octave, terminating on the trite hyperbolaeon [f]. The seventh is the Mixolydian; it is formed from the seventh species of octave and comes to a close on the paranete hyperbolaeon [g].

A single doubling, that is, an octave, can accommodate no additional species because it is made up of eight pitches; this is so because every interval has one more pitch than it has species. (Hence Ptolemy added an eighth mode, the Hypermixolydian, forming it from the properties of the second and third modes.)[5] Thus the fourth has four strings and three species, the fifth has five strings and four species, and the octave has eight strings and seven species.

Finally, the first species of fourth has its semitone at its third step; the second species at its second step; and the third at its first.[6] And the same species always

1. There is something of a pun here: *modus* means both measure and character or manner.
2. The duple proportion (2:1) produces the octave; the triple (3:1), the tenth; the quadruple (4:1), the double octave; the sesquialtera (3:2), the fifth; and the sesquitertial (4:3), the fourth.
3. The "notes of the fifteen strings" refers to the fifteen notes of the Greek Greater Perfect System as it appears in Boethius; the notes were named for finger positions upon the strings of a lyre or kithara. The *Alia musica* uses these note names as did Hucbald's *De harmonica institutione;* in the present translation they will be followed by their letter equivalents in brackets, with upper case letters for the lower octave and lower case for the upper octave.
4. That is, it extends from A upward to a. The author of this portion of the treatise, which functions perhaps as an introduction to the whole, numbers the modes according to their ascending position on the Greek Greater Perfect System. In doing so the author is depending upon Boethius; in the main body of the treatise the modes are given their familiar medieval numbering.
5. The difficulty with an eighth mode within this context is, of course, that it has the same octave species as the first. The main body of the treatise, however, distinguishes between the first and eighth modes by their governing notes (their finals). Indeed the eighth mode is given the ambitus D to d, with a governing note of G, thus creating a proper tetrardus plagal; still Ptolemy's name for it, the hypermixolydian, is retained rather than the eventual hypomixolydian. See Heard, 65–67.
6. Counting downward, with the first species beginning on a.

returns at the fourth place, whether as a disjunct or conjunct tetrachord;[7] while the same species of fifth does not return at every fifth place.[8] It follows from this that by adding one whole tone the three species of fourth constitute the first three species of fifth; while the fourth species of fifth ends with a semitone (the first species begins at the nete diezeugmenon [e]).[9]

It remains only to examine the properties of the various octave species. The first species has its semitones at the third and sixth step;[10] the second at the fourth and seventh; the third at the first and fifth; the fourth at the second and sixth; the fifth at the third and seventh; the sixth at the first and fourth; the seventh at the second and fifth; and the eighth, as with the first species, at the third and sixth.

To return, in conclusion, to these same octave species, since the lichanos hypaton [D] is the proslambanomenos [D] of the Dorian,[11] the mese of the Dorian [a], which is the paranete diezeugmenon [a] of the Hypodorian, is an integral fourth higher than the mese [e] of the same Hypodorian. The difference between the Phrygian and Hypophrygian is similar, as is that between the Lydian and Hypolydian; while the Mixolydian differs from the Hypermixolydian by only a tone.

7. Chailley's punctuation, pp. 108–109, is preferred here to that of Gerbert and Heard, placing *quintis locis* with the following sentence. But Chailley's interpretation of the passage, which considers the author of the treatise guilty of absurdity, may be too complicated. The author's statement offers less difficulty when viewed within the context of the Greater Perfect System:

8. Obviously not, within a system that is made up of similar tetrachords.
9. The fourth species of fifth, from b to E, consists in a tritone plus a semitone.
10. That is, the third and the sixth step counting downward, etc.
11. The author's concern is with octave species species rather than fixed positions on the Greater Perfect System. Thus the proslambanomenos of the Dorian is (by affinity to A, the proslambanomenos of the Hypodorian) its lowest note, D; and, in the following clause, the paranete diezeugmenon of the Hypodorian is (by affinity to d, the paranete diezeugmenon of the Dorian) that mode's highest note, a.

18 Pseudo-Odo of Cluny

The *Dialogue on Music,* referred to also as the *Enchiridion musices* ("Musical Handbook"), was until recently attributed to the celebrated Benedictine abbot, Odo of Cluny (c. 878–942); the attribution stemmed from a reference in the treatise to a Dom Odo, now identified as the later-tenth-century Odo of Arezzo (see note 6). The *Dialogue* is the work of an anonymous theorist writing in the diocese of Milan sometime early in the eleventh century. The work is significant, among other reasons, for its use of letter notation with repeated octaves beginning on A, its paradigmatic description of the eight ecclesiastical modes, and its influence on Guido of Arezzo.

The treatise's Prologue, frequently appearing with it in manuscripts, is actually the work of another anonymous author. Originating in the same Italian milieu as the *Dialogue,* it was meant to serve as a preface to an antiphoner using an alphabetical notation similar to that advocated in the Dialogue; it, too, had a demonstrable influence upon Guido. Thus, the anonymous authors of the *Dialogue* and the Prologue, Odo of Arezzo, and the culminating figure of Guido, constitute an important Italian school of musical theorists.

Dialogue on Music

PROLOGUE

You have insistently requested, beloved brothers, that I should communicate to you a few rules concerning music, these to be only of a sort which boys and simple persons may understand and by means of which, with God's help, they may quickly attain to perfect skill in singing. You asked this, having yourselves seen and heard and having verified by certain evidence that it could be done. Indeed, when I lived among you, I instructed, with no help other than that of God, certain of your boys and young men in this art. Some of them after three days of training in it, others after four days, and others after a single week, were able to learn several antiphons and in a short time to sing them without hesitation, although they had not heard them sung by anyone, but were content simply with a copy written according to our rules. With the passage of not many more days they were singing at first sight, extempore, and without a mistake any written music, something which until now ordinary singers had never been able to do, with many of them continuing in vain to practice and study singing for fifty years.

When you earnestly and diligently inquired whether our doctrines would be of value for all melodies, I took as my helper a certain brother who seemed perfect in comparison with other singers, and I investigated together with him the Antiphoner of the blessed Gregory, where I found that nearly everything was accurately recorded. A few items, corrupted by unskilled singers, were corrected, both on the evidence of other singers and by the authority of the rules. But on very rare occasion within the longer melodies we found notes belonging to another mode, notes, that is, which contravened the rules by being too high or too low. Yet, since universal usage agreed in defending these

TEXT: The text of the Dialogue proper is from Martin Gerbert, ed., *Scriptores ecclesiastici de musica* (St. Blasien, 1784), vol. 1, pp. 25–59, 263–64; the text of the Prologue is from Michel Huglo, "Der Prolog des Odo zugeschriebenen 'Dialogus de Musica,'" *Archiv für Musikwissenschaft* 28 (1971): 138–39. Translation by William Strunk, Jr., and Oliver Strunk, revised by James McKinnon.

chants, we did not presume to emend them.[1] We marked them as unusual, however, in order that no one inquiring into the truth of the rule might be left in doubt.

This done, you were kindled by a greater desire and insisted, with passionate entreaties and urgings, not only that there be rules, but also that the whole Antiphoner should be written in practical notation and with the formulas of the tones,[2] to the honor of God and of his most holy mother Mary, in whose venerable monastery this project was proceeding.

Deriving confidence, therefore, from your entreaties, and complying with the orders of our common father, I am neither willing nor able to discontinue this work. There is among the learned of this age a very difficult and extensive doctrine of this art, but let whoever pleases cultivate and rework the field with great effort. He who of himself perceives our little gift of God will be satisfied with a simple fruit. And in order that you may better understand it and be adequately recompensed for your good will, let one of yours approach me to converse and ask questions. I shall not neglect to respond to him in so far as the Lord has given me the power.

1. OF THE MONOCHORD AND ITS USE

(Disciple) What is music?
(Master) The science of singing truly and the easy road to perfection in singing.
(D) How so?
(M) As the teacher first shows you all the letters on a slate, so the musician introduces all the sounds of melody on the monochord.
(D) What is the monochord?
(M) It is a long rectangular wooden chest, hollow within like a cithara; upon it is mounted a string, by the sounding of which you easily understand the varieties of sounds.
(D) How is the string itself mounted?
(M) A straight line is drawn down the middle of the chest, lengthwise, and points are marked on the line at a distance of one inch from each end. In the spaces outside these points two end-pieces are set, which hold the string so suspended above the line that the line beneath the string is of the same length as the string between the two end-pieces.
(D) How does one string produce many different sounds?
(M) The letters, or notes, used by musicians are placed in order on the line beneath the string, and when the bridge is moved between the line and the string, shortening or lengthening it, the string marvelously reproduces any chant by means of these letters. When the boys mark some antiphon with these

1. It is interesting indeed that the author appears to favor the preservation of the traditional chant melodies over the demands of modal theory.
2. For the "formulas of the tones," see David Hiley, *Western Plainchant: A Handbook* (Oxford: Clarendon Press, 1993), pp. 331–33.

letters, they learn it better and more easily from the string than if they heard some one sing it; and they are able after a few months' training to discard the string and sing by sight alone, without hesitation, music that they have never heard.

(D) What you say is truly marvelous; our singers have never aspired to such perfection.

(M) Instead, brother, they missed the right path, and failing to ask the way, they labored all their life in vain.

(D) How can it be true that a string teaches better than a man?

(M) A man sings as he will or can, but the string is divided with such art by very learned men, using the aforesaid letters, that if it is diligently observed and considered, it cannot mislead.

2. OF THE MEASUREMENT OF THE MONOCHORD

(D) I ask, then, what this art is.

(M) The measurement of the monochord, for if it is well measured, it never deceives.

(D) Can I possibly learn these measurements, simply and in a few words?

(M) Today, with God's help; only listen diligently.

At the first end-piece of the monochord, the point of which we have spoken above, place the letter Γ, that is, a Greek G (this Γ, since it is a letter rarely used, is by many not understood). Carefully divide the distance from Γ to the point placed at the other end into nine parts, and where the first ninth from Γ ends, write the letter A; we shall call this the first step. Then, similarly, divide the distance from the first letter, A, to the end into nine, and at the first ninth, place the letter B for the second step. Then return to the beginning, divide by four from Γ, and for the third step write the letter C. From the first letter, A, divide similarly by four, and for the fourth step write the letter D. In the same way, dividing by four from B, you will find the fifth step, E. The third letter, C, likewise reveals the sixth step, F. Then return to Γ, and from it and from the other letters that follow it in order, divide the line in two parts, that is, in the middle, until you have fourteen or fifteen steps not counting Γ.[3]

When you divide the sounds in the middle, you must mark them differently. For example, when you bisect the distance from Γ, instead of Γ, write G; for A bisected, set down a second a; for B, a second ♮; for C, a second c; for D, a second d; for E, a second e; for F, a second f; for G, a second g; and for a, a second ♮a; so that from the middle of the monochord forward, the letters will be the same as in the first part.[4]

3. The explanation is complete except for one detail. If one does not count Γ, then there are fifteen steps if one counts A, and fourteen if one does not.

4. One must not be misled here into thinking that the second octave, because it begins in the middle of the string, will fill the second half of the string. It will occupy only half the space of the first octave, thus leaving room for a theoretically infinite series of higher octaves, each higher octave taking up half of the remaining string length.

In addition, from the sixth step, F, divide into four, and before ♮, place a second round b; these two are taken as a single step, one being called the second ninth step; both are not regularly found together in the same chant.

The figures, both sounds and letters, are thus arranged in order:

	Γ		
First step	A	Eighth step	a
Second step	B	First ninth step	b
		Second ninth step	♮
Third step	C	Tenth step	c
Fourth step	D	Eleventh step	d
Fifth step	E	Twelfth step	e
Sixth step	F	Thirteenth step	f
Seventh step	G	Fourteenth step	g
		Fifteenth step	a

(D) Thanks be to God, I understand well, and I am confident that I shall now know how to make a monochord.

3. OF TONE AND SEMITONE

But why is it, I ask, that I see on the regularly measured monochord in one place smaller and in another place larger spaces and intervals between the steps?

(M) The greater space is called a tone; it is from Γ to the first step, A, and from the first step, A, to the second, B. The lesser space, such as that from the second step, B, to the third, C, is called a semitone and makes a more restricted rise and fall. By no measure or number may the space of a semitone amount to that of a tone, but when the divisions are made in their places by the calculations given above, tones and semitones are formed.

If you have marked all the tones to the very last step, you will marvel to find in every one of them a ninefold division just as you found it at first from Γ to the first step, A, and from the first step, A, to the second, B. Yet the first and second ninth steps, b and ♮, form with respect to one another neither a tone nor a semitone, but from the first ninth step, b, to the eighth, a, is a semitone and to the tenth, c, a tone; conversely, from the second ninth step, ♮, to the eighth, a, is a tone and to the tenth, c, a semitone. Thus one of them is always superfluous, and in any chant you accept one and reject the other in order not to seem to be making a tone and a semitone in the same place, which would be absurd.

(D) It is especially surprising that, although I did not divide by nine, except from Γ to the first step, A, and from the first step, A, to the second, B, I have found that all the tones are equally based on a ninefold division. But show me, if you please, whether there are other divisions of the monochord and whether they are found in all or in several places.

4. OF THE CONSONANCES

(M) Besides the division of the tone, there are three divisions that govern the natural position of sounds which I have spoken of above. The first is the quaternary division, as from the first step, A, to the fourth, D, so called because it is a division by four; this has four pitches and three intervals, namely, two tones and one semitone. Therefore, wherever you find two tones and a semitone between two pitches on the monochord, you will discover on trial that the interval formed by these two pitches maintains itself in quaternary division to the very end of the string; for this reason it is called *diatessaron* [fourth], that is, "of four."

The second is the ternary division, as from the first step, A, to the fifth, E, this contains five pitches and four intervals, namely, three tones and one semitone. Therefore, wherever you see three tones and one semitone between two pitches, the interval formed by these two pitches will be maintained to the end of the string by successive divisions of one-third. This interval is called *diapente* [fifth], that is, "of five," because it encloses five pitches.

The third is what is divided by two, or in the middle; it is called *diapason* [octave], that is, "of all." This, as was said above, you will plainly recognize from the likeness of the letters, as from the first step, A, to the eighth, a. It consists of eight pitches and seven intervals, namely, of five tones and two semitones, for it contains one fourth and one fifth, the interval from the first step, A, to the fourth, D, forming a fourth, that from the fourth step, D, to the eighth, a, forming a fifth. From the first step, A, to the eighth, a, the octave takes on this form: A, B, C, D, E, F, G, a.

(D) In a few words I have learned not a little about divisions. Now I wish to hear why the same letters are used both in the first and in the second part.

(M) The reason is, that since the sounds of the second part, beginning with the seventh step, G (but excepting the first ninth step, b), are formed from those of the first part by the octave, both parts so agree with each other that whatever letters form a tone, semitone, fourth, fifth, or octave in the first part will likewise be found to do so in the second part. For example, in the first part, from Γ to A is a tone, to B is a tone and a tone, that is, a *ditone* [major third], to C a fourth, to D a fifth, to G an octave; similarly, in the second part, from G to a is a tone, to ♮ is a tone and a tone, to c a fourth, to d a fifth, to g an octave. From this it follows that every melody is similarly sung in the first and in the second part. And the sounds of the first part sound in concord with those of the second part, as men's voices with those of boys.

(D) I consider that this has been wisely done. Now I expect to hear first how I may note down a chant so that I may understand it without a teacher and so that, when you give me examples of the rules, I may recognize the chant better and, if anything completely escapes my memory, have recourse to such notes with entire confidence.

(M) Place before your eyes the letters of the monochord as the melody ranges through them; then, if you do not fully recognize the force of the letters themselves, you may, by striking the string at the place of the letters, hear them and learn them, wonderful to relate, from a master without his knowing it.

(D) Indeed, I must say that you have given me a wonderful master, who, made by me, teaches me, and teaching me, knows nothing himself. Indeed, I fervently embrace him for his patience and obedience; he will sing to me whenever I wish, and he will never torment me with blows or abuse when provoked by the slowness of my sense.

(M) He is a good master, but he demands a diligent listener.

5. OF THE CONJUNCTIONS OF SOUNDS

(D) To what am I to direct especial diligence?

(M) To the conjunctions of sounds which form the various consonances, so that, just as they are various and different, you may be able to express each of them conveniently in a dissimilar and different manner.

(D) I ask that you teach me how many differences there are and that you demonstrate them to me by examples in everyday use.

(M) There are six, both in descent and in ascent. The first conjunction of sounds is that where we join two sounds between which there is one semitone, as from the fifth step, E, to the sixth, F, a consonance closer and more restricted than any other; for example, the first ascent of the antiphon *Haec est quae nescivit* or, in descent, conversely, *Vidimus stellam.* The second is that where there is a tone between two sounds, as from the third step, C, to the fourth, D; in ascent: *Non vos relinquam* and in descent: *Angelus Domini.* The third is that where a tone and a semitone make the difference between two sounds, as between the fourth step, D, and the sixth, F; in ascent: *Joannes autem* and in descent: *In lege.* The fourth is that where there are two tones between one sound and another, as from the sixth step, F, to the eighth, a; in ascent: *Adhuc multa habeo* and in descent: *Ecce Maria.* The fifth is that created by the fourth, as from the first step, A, to the fourth, D; in ascent: *Valde honorandus* and in descent: *Secundum autem.* The sixth is that created by the fifth, as from the fourth step, D, to the eighth, a, thus: *Primum quaerite,* or, in descent, from the seventh step, G, to the third, C, thus: *Canite tuba.* Other regular conjunctions of sounds are nowhere to be found.[5]

Haec est quae ne - sci - vit   Vi - di - mus stel - lam   e - jus

5. In Gerbert's edition, the incipits of the various melodies cited in this chapter are printed (sometimes incorrectly) in letters immediately above the textual incipits. Strunk replaced these with musical notation derived from modern chant books.

Non   vos   re - lin - quam

An - ge - lus Do - mi - ni nun - ti - a - vit

Jo - han - nes au - tem cum au - dis - set

In   le - ge   Do - mi - ni

Ad - huc mul - ta   ha - be - o

Ec - ce   Ma - ri - a   ge - nu - it

Val - de   ho - no - ran - dus   est

Se - cun - dum   au - tem   si - mi - le   est   hu - ic

Pri - mum quae - ri - te   re - gnum De - i

Ca - ni - te   tu - ba   in   Sy - on

6. Of the Distinguishing of Tone And Semitone According to the Modes

Mediocre singers often fall into the greatest error because they scarcely consider the qualities of tone and semitone and of the other consonances. Each of them chooses what first pleases his ear or appears easiest to learn and to perform, so that a considerable error is made with respect to the mode of many chants. (I use the term "mode" for the set of eight modes or tones, by the formulas of which all chants are arranged; for if I said "tone," it would be uncertain whether I was speaking of the tones of the formulas or of the tones formed by ninefold disposition and division.) These singers, if you question them about the mode of any chant, promptly reply with what they do not know as though they knew it perfectly. But if you ask them how they know it, they say falteringly: "Because at the beginning and end it is like other chants of the same mode," although they do not know the mode of any melody at all. They do not know that a dissimilarity in a single pitch forces the mode to change, as in the antiphon *O beatum Pontificem,* which, although in the second mode at the beginning and end, was most painstakingly emended to the first mode by Dom Odo,[6] merely because of the ascending interval on which are sung the words *O Martine dulcedo.* You can examine this more thoroughly in the antiphon *Domine qui operati sunt,* for if you begin, as many attempt to, on F, in the sixth mode, it will not depart from that mode until the semitone, at *in tabernaculo tuo,* on one syllable.[7] Yet since it is thus in use, and sounds well, it ought not to be emended.[8] But let us inquire whether it might not begin in another mode, in which all will be found consonant and in which there will be no need for emendation. Begin it, then, on G, that is, in the eighth mode, and you will find that it stands regularly in that mode. For this reason, some begin *Domine* as in *Amen dico vobis.*[9]

From this it is understood that the musician who lightly and presumptuously emends many melodies is ignorant unless he first goes through all the modes to determine whether the melody may perhaps not stand in one or another, nor should he care as much for its similarity to other melodies as for its fidelity to the rules. But if it conforms to no mode, let it be emended according to the one with which it least disagrees. This also should be observed: that the emended melody either sound better or depart little from its previous likeness. (D) You have warned me well against the error of unskilled singers and have also given me in few words no little knowledge of the careful investigation of the regulated monochord, of the verification of regular melodies and the emendation of false ones—all matters that provide a useful and appropriate exercise of one's mind.

7. OF THE LIMITS OF THE MODES

(D) Tell me, now, of how many sounds ought a melody to be formed.
(M) Some say eight, others nine, others ten.

---

6. The Odo in question here is not Odo of Cluny, but probably Odo of Arezzo, the later-tenth-century author of an antiphoner using alphabetic notation and of an explanatory treatise; see Michel Huglo, *Les Tonaires* (Paris: Société Française de Musicologie, 1971), 182–85.
7. The antiphon as it appears below in the version from the Worcester antiphoner illustrates the author's concern; if the antiphon begins on F, rather than transposed to c as it is here, the a and b-flat would appear as D and E-flat. The E-flat of course lies outside the contemporary gamut, and also creates an octave species on F identical to that normally found on G, thus violating modal theory in a fundamental way.

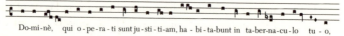

Do-mi-nè, qui o - pe - ra - ti sunt ju - sti - ti-am, ha - bi - ta-bunt in ta-ber-na-cu-lo   tu - o,

8. See note 1 above.
9. The typical eighth mode version of *Amen [amen] dico vobis* begins thus:

8. G

A   - men, a - men di - co vo - bis,   qui - a plo - rá - bi - tis et flé -

(D) Why eight?

(M) Because of the greater division, that is, the octave, or because the citharas of the ancients had eight strings.

(D) Why nine?

(M) Because of the double fifth, which is bounded by nine pitches. For since from Γ to the fourth step, D, is one fifth, and from this same fourth step to the eighth, a, is another; from Γ to the eighth step, a, there are nine pitches.

(D) Why ten?

(M) Because of the authority of David's psaltery, or because the triple fourth is found at the tenth pitch. For from Γ to the third step, C, is one fourth, from the third step, C, to the sixth, F, is a second, from the sixth step, F, to the first ninth, b, is a third; from Γ, therefore, to the first ninth step, b, one counts ten pitches.

(D) May there also be fewer sounds in a melody?

(M) There may indeed be five or four, so situated, however, that the five produce the fifth and the four the fourth.

(D) The reasoning you have adduced and the evidence of nearly all melodies proves that what you say is true. Now explain what tone is, that which you more often call mode.

8. WHAT MODE IS, AND WHENCE IT IS DETERMINED OR DISTINGUISHED

(M) A tone, or mode, is a rule which classifies every chant by its final. For unless you know the final you cannot know where the chant ought to begin or how far it ought to ascend and descend.

(D) What rule does the beginning take from the final?

(M) Every beginning ought to concord with its final in one of the before-mentioned six consonances. No note may begin a chant, unless it be the final itself or be consonant with it in some one of these six consonances. And whatever notes agree with the final by means of these same six consonances may also begin a melody having this final; with the exception that a melody ending on the fifth step, E, the first of the semitones in the third mode, is often found to begin on the tenth step, c, which is removed from the fifth step, E, by a fifth plus a semitone.

The distinctions, too, that is, the places at which we pause in a chant and at which we divide it, ought obviously to end in each mode on the same notes on which a chant in that mode may begin. And where each mode best and most often begins, there as a rule it best and most suitably begins and ends its distinctions. Several distinctions ought to end on the note which concludes the mode, the masters teach, for if more distinctions are made on some other note than on this one, they expect the chant to end on that other note and insist that it be changed from the mode in which it was. A chant, in other words, belongs for the most part to the mode in which the majority of its distinctions lie. The beginnings, too, are found most often and most suitably on the note which concludes the chant. You may confirm what has been said by the example of the antiphon *Tribus miraculis: Tribus miraculis* is the first distinction; *ornatum diem sanctum colimus* the second; *hodie stella Magos duxit ad praesepium* the third; *hodie vinum ex aqua factum est ad nuptias* the fourth; and *hodie a Joanne Christus baptizari voluit* is the last.[10] So you see that in a properly regulated chant several distinctions begin and end within its own mode and that chants begin and end on the same note.

9. ON THE RANGE OF THE MODES

(D) That these things are as you say is everywhere supported by the authority of singing masters. But continue: what rule with regard to ascent and descent does a chant take from its final?

(M) As for acute or high chants, as in the first, third, fifth, and seventh modes, none ought to ascend further above its final than to the eighth note, the pitch having the same letter as the final, and this because of the special quality of the division which we call the octave. A chant of this sort extends one note below its final. In lower chants, as in the second, fourth, sixth, and eighth modes, there should be no descent below the final to a note not joined to it by means of one of the six before-mentioned consonances; in ascent the range is from the final by means of these same six consonances to the fifth sound, indeed sometimes as far as the sixth. On what notes the chants of all modes most often begin (according to present usage), you will observe from their formulas.

10. THE EIGHT MODES

(D) Now that you have shown how the chants of all the modes are regulated by the final, it is time to explain how many modes, or tones, there are.

(M) Some count four modes.

(D) For what reason?

(M) Because every properly regulated chant ends on one of four pitches of the monochord.

(D) Which pitches are these?

(M) The fourth step, D, on which concludes the mode that we call *authentus protus,* that is, the first author or leader; the fifth step, E, on which concludes the mode that we call *authentus deuterus,* the second author or leader; the sixth step, F, on which concludes the *authentus tritus,* the third author or leader; and the seventh step, G, on which concludes the *authentus tetrardus,* the fourth author or leader. These four, moreover, are divided into eight.

---

10. Tribus miraculis is the *Magnificat* antiphon for second vespers of the Epiphany. It has six cadential points, the five interior ones given here and the one at the end of the final phrase, *ut salvaret nos alleluia;* in the Vatican editions it is a first mode chant with all of its phrases ending on D except for the one ending with the words *baptizari voluit.*

(D) For what reason?

(M) For the sake of high and low chants. For when a chant in the authentus protus is acute or high, we call the mode the authentus protus. But if in the same authentus protus it is grave or low, we call it the *plaga proti.*

(D) Why plaga proti?

(M) Plaga proti, or "a part of the first," because it ends on the same part, that is, on the same place or step of the monochord on which the authentus protus ended, the fourth, D. In a similar way, when a chant in the authentus deuterus is acute we call it the authentus deuterus, but if it is grave we call it the *plaga deuteri.* In the same manner, we say of the authentus tritus, *plaga triti,* and of the authentus tetrardus, *plaga tetrardi.* Common usage, however, has taught us to say first and second mode instead of authentus protus and plaga proti; third and fourth mode instead of authentus deuterus and plaga deuteri; fifth and sixth mode instead of authentus tritus and its plaga; and seventh and eighth mode instead of authentus tetrardus and its plaga. There are eight modes, then, by means of which every melody, proceeding by one of eight different sets of characteristics, is distinguished.

(D) In what way might I be able to to perceive their divergent and common qualities?

(M) By means of tones and semitones. For where tones and semitones occur in similar order, there also the remaining consonances are formed alike. Wherever there are two tones and a semitone, there will also be a fourth, and wherever three tones and a semitone are grouped together, there also the fifth will not be wanting. The remaining consonances are to be understood in a similar way.

·   ·   ·   ·   ·

(D) Since I can hardly find even a few melodies which violate these rules, I have no doubt that their scarcity and, so to speak, furtive singularity are the work of presumptuous and corrupt singers.

(M) A rule, certainly, is a general mandate of any art; thus things that are singular do not obey the rules of art.

(D) But please add a few things more about the law of the modes, with respect to the position of each note.

(M) Your request deserves an answer, for with each note there is some affinity to one of the aforesaid modes.[11]

For example, Γ, since it has above it two tones, and after these a semitone and two tones and then a semitone and a tone, rightly bears a similarity to the seventh mode, for the final of the seventh mode sounds at the octave to Γ. Likewise the first step, A, since it has below it a tone, and above it a tone, a

---

11. There follows one of the earlier discussions of the so-called affinities, although the author uses the term *similitudo* rather than *affinitas;* on the history of the concept see Dolores Pesce, *The Affinities and Medieval Transposition* (Bloomington: Indiana University Press, 1987).

semitone, and two tones, observes the rule of the first mode and therefore is referred to with good reason as the first mode. And the second step, B, since one descends below it by two tones and ascends above it by a semitone and two tones, obeys the usual rule of the fourth mode. In addition, the third step, C, since it has below it a semitone and two tones, and above it two tones, a semitone, and then three tones, maintains the character of the fifth and sixth modes.

We say that the eighth step, a, occupies the first place in similarity to the first step, whose octave it is. On the other hand, if you consider it in connection with the first ninth step, b-flat, it will have in descent a tone, but in ascent a semitone and three tones, like the third mode. The first ninth step, b-flat, has below it a semitone and two tones, like the sixth mode, and above it—either because there are three tones in succession, or rather because it is not joined by any affinity to the following fourth (the principal consonance)—it has no regular resemblance to any mode. Nor can it form an octave with the notes that come after it; consequently you will find that neither a melody nor a distinction may begin or end with it, except by a fault.[12] The second ninth step, ♮, like the second step, B, resembles the fourth mode. The tenth step, c, like the third step, C, agrees with the fifth or sixth mode. But if it be deprived of the second ninth step, ♮, it will have below it a tone, a semitone, and two tones, and above it two tones and a semitone, like the eighth mode, from whose final it marks a fourth.

The remaining sounds are easily dealt with because of the similarity of their letters, as this diagram shows:

					III								
VII	I		V	I	III V	VII	I		V	I	III V	VII	I
Γ	A	B	C	D	E F	G	a ♮		c	d	e f	g	a a
VIII	II	IV	VI	II	IV VI	VIII	II	IV	VI		II IV VI	VIII	II
						VIII							

From what has been said, the diligent inquirer will, with the aid of divine grace, understand many other matters both concerning the modes and concerning the remaining rules of this art. But if he is negligent, or if he should presumptuously think that he understands them by the keenness of his wit and not by divine enlightenment, either he will comprehend them not at all or, so long as he does not return thanks to the Giver, he will become, God forbid, more the vassal of his pride than the servant of his Creator, who is blessed, world without end. Amen.

12. The language dealing with b-flat here is obscure, perhaps corrupt in places, but the overall sense is clear. There can be no affinities with the series of pitches beginning with b-flat at the ninth step of the gamut for two reasons: the first four steps of the series constitute a tritone, not a fourth, and the b-flat creates an octave with neither the B at the second step of the gamut, nor with any b-flat above, since the gamut runs out at aa.

19 Guido of Arezzo

Guido, born probably toward the end of the tenth century, was educated in the Benedictine Abbey of Pomposa on the Adriatic coast near Ferrara. There he and his colleague Michael began an antiphoner, now lost, that employed the unique style of notation described in the Prologue translated here. Around 1025 Guido moved to Arezzo to train the singers of its cathedral. His celebrated treatise, the *Micrologus,* was commissioned by Theodaldus, bishop of Arezzo between 1023 and 1036. Guido, by then a renowned pedagogue of ecclesiastical chant, was called to Rome by Pope John XIX around 1028; he left after a short stay and settled in a monastery near Arezzo, possibly the Camaldolese foundation at Avellana. His death date is unknown.

Although it may be an exaggeration to credit Guido with the invention of the staff, the Prologue to his Antiphoner makes it clear that he was at least a key figure in its early development; the precise date of the Prologue's composition is not known, but it is generally believed to have been written sometime after completion of the antiphoner, perhaps about 1030. A second famous innovation of Guido, the use of solmization syllables, is described in his *Epistolo de ignoto cantu,* the second reading to be translated here. The Epistle, which mentions the Prologue, was written sometime before the death of Pope John XIX in 1033. In subsequent centuries, Guido's reputation achieved mythic proportions, but there is no denying that he was a musical theorist of singular intelligence and originality.

Prologue to His Antiphoner

In our times singers are the most foolish of all men. For in any art those things which we know of ourselves are much more numerous than those which we learn from a master. Small boys know the meanings of all books as soon as they have read the Psalter attentively. Rustics grasp the science of agriculture unthinkingly, for he who knows how to prune one vineyard, to plant one tree, to load one ass, performs without hesitation in all cases just as he did in the one, or even better. But the wretched singers and their pupils, though they sing every day for a hundred years, will never sing by themselves without a master a single antiphon, not even a short one—thus losing time enough in singing to have learned thoroughly both sacred and secular letters.

And what is the most perilous of all evils, many clerics under religious rule[1]

TEXT: Joseph Smits van Waesberghe, ed., *Guidonis "Prologus in Antiphonarium,"* Divitiae Musicae Artis A.III (Buren: Frits Knuf, 1975). Translation by Oliver Strunk, revised by James McKinnon.

1. *Religiosi ordinis clerici,* an apparent reference to canons, that is, secular clergy who live under a quasi-monastic discipline, including the obligation to sing the daily Office.

and monks neglect the Psalms, the sacred readings, the nocturnal vigils, and the other works of piety that arouse and lead us on to everlasting glory, while they apply themselves with unceasing and most foolish effort to the science of singing which they can never master.

Who does not bewail this also, which is at once a grave error and a dangerous discord in Holy Church, that when we celebrate the Divine Office we are often seen rather to strive among ourselves than to praise God? One scarcely agrees with another, neither the pupil with his master, nor the pupil with his colleague. It is for this reason that the antiphoners are not one, nor yet a few, but rather as many as there are the masters in the various churches; and that the antiphoner is now commonly said to be, not Gregory's, but Leo's, or Albert's, or someone's else. And since to learn one is most difficult, there can be no doubt that to learn many is impossible.

Since the masters, then, change many things arbitrarily, little or no blame should attach to me if I depart only in the slightest from common use so that every chant may return uniformly to a common rule of art. And inasmuch as all these evils and many others have arisen from the fault of those who make antiphoners, I strongly urge and maintain that no one should henceforth presume to provide an antiphoner with neumes unless he understands this art and knows how to do it according to the rules laid down here. Otherwise, without having first been a disciple of truth, he will most certainly be a master of error.

Therefore I have decided, with God's help, to write this antiphoner in such a way that hereafter any intelligent and studious person may learn the chant by means of it; after he has thoroughly learned a part of it through a master, he will unhesitatingly understand the rest of it by himself without one. Should anyone doubt that I am telling the truth, let him come to learn and see that small boys can do this under our direction, boys who until now have been beaten for their gross ignorance of the Psalms and vulgar letters. Often they do not know how to pronounce the words and syllables of the very antiphon which they sing correctly by themselves without a master, something which, with God's help, any intelligent and studious person will be able to do if he tries to understand with what great care we have arranged the neumes.

The notes are so arranged, then, that each sound, however often it may be repeated in a melody, is found always in its own row. And in order that you may better distinguish these rows, lines are drawn close together, and some rows of sounds occur on the lines themselves, others in the intervening intervals or spaces. All the sounds on one line or in one space sound alike. And in order that you may understand to which lines or spaces each sound belongs, certain letters of the monochord are written at the beginning of the lines or spaces. And the lines are also gone over in colors, thereby indicating that in the whole antiphoner and in every melody those lines or spaces which have one and the same letter or color, however many they may be, sound alike throughout, as though all were on one line. For just as the line indicates complete identity of sounds, so the letter or color indicates complete identity of lines, and hence of sounds also.

Then if you find the second row of sounds everywhere distinguished by such a letter or colored line, you will also know readily that this same identity of sounds and neumes runs through all the second rows. Understand the same of the third, fourth, and remaining rows, whether you count up or down. It is then most certainly true that all neumes or sounds similarly positioned on lines of the same letter or color sound alike throughout, and they do so even if differently shaped so long as the line has the same letter or color; while on different lines or in different spaces even similarly formed neumes sound not at all alike. Hence, however perfect the formation of the neumes might be, it is altogether meaningless and worthless without the addition of letters or colors.

We use two colors, namely yellow and red, and by means of them I teach you a very useful rule that will enable you to know readily to what tone and to what letter of the monochord every neume and any sound belongs; that is, if— as is greatly convenient—you make frequent use of the monochord and of the formulas of the modes.

Now, as I shall show fully later on, the letters of the monochord are seven. Wherever, then, you see the color yellow, there is the third letter [C], and wherever you see the color red, there is the sixth letter [F], whether these colors be on the lines or between them. Hence in the third row beneath the yellow is the first letter [A], belonging to the first and second mode; above this, next to the yellow, is the second letter [B], belonging to the third and fourth mode; then, on the yellow itself, is the third letter or sound [C], belonging to the fifth and sixth mode; immediately above the yellow and third below the red is the fourth letter [D], belonging to the first and second mode; nearest the red is the fifth letter [E], belonging to the third and fourth mode; on the red itself is the sixth letter [F], belonging to the fifth and sixth mode; next above the red is the seventh letter [G], belonging to the seventh and eighth mode; then, in the third row above the red, below the yellow, is repeated the first letter [a], belonging, as already explained, to the first and second mode; after this all the rest are repeated, differing in no respect from the foregoing; all of which this diagram will teach you quite clearly.

VII	I	III	V	I	III	V	VII	I	III	V	I	III	V	VII	I	III	V	I
															a ♮		c	d
Γ	A	B	C	D	E	F	G	a ♮		c	d	e		f	g	a ♮	c	d
VIII	II	IV	VI	II	IV	VI	VIII	II	IV	VI	II	IV	VI	VIII	II	IV	VI	II

Although each letter or sound belongs always to two modes, the formulas of the second, fourth, six, and eighth modes agree much better and more frequently in the single neumes or sounds, for the formulas of the first, third, fifth, and seventh agree only when the melody, descending from above, concludes with a low note.[2]

Know, finally, that if you would make progress with these notes, you must learn by heart a fair number of melodies so that by the memory of these particular neumes, modes, and notes you will recognize all sounds, of whatever sort. For it is indeed quite another thing to recall something with understanding than it is to sing something by rote; only the wise can do the former while persons without foresight can often do the latter.

Let this suffice for a basic understanding of the neumes for the unsophisticated. As to how sounds are liquescent; whether they should be sung connected or separate; which are retarded and tremulous, and which hastened; how a chant is divided by distinctions; whether the following or preceding sound be higher, lower, or equal sounding; by a simple discussion all this is revealed in the very shape of the neumes, if the neumes are, as they should be, carefully composed.

2. To put it differently, the final will, as a rule, occur more frequently in plagal melodies than in authentic ones. Thus a given step will show a greater correspondence to the appropriate plagal formula than to the authentic formula with which it is paired.

20 Guido of Arezzo

Epistle Concerning an Unknown Chant

TO THE MOST BLESSED AND BELOVED BROTHER MICHAEL, GUIDO, BY MANY VICISSITUDES CAST DOWN AND STRENGTHENED.

Either the times are hard or the judgments of the divine ordinance are obscure when truth is trampled upon by falsehood and love is trampled upon by envy (which rarely ceases to accompany our order); thus the conspiring of the Philistines punishes the Israelitish transgression, so that if anything should turn out according to our wishes, the mortal soul would perish in its self-confidence. For our actions are truly good only when we ascribe to the Creator all that we are able to accomplish.

Hence it is that you see me banished from pleasant domains and yourself so choked by the snares of the envious that you can scarcely breathe. In this I find that we are much like a certain artisan who presented to Augustus Caesar an incomparable treasure, namely, flexible glass. Thinking that he deserved a

TEXT: Martin Gerbert, ed., *Epistola de ignoto cantu. Scriptores ecclestiastici de musica* (St. Blasien, 1784), vol. 2, pp. 42–46, 50. Translation by Oliver Strunk, revised by James McKinnon.

reward beyond all others because he could do something beyond the power of all others, he was by a cruel reversal of fortune sentenced to death, lest, if the glass could be made as durable as it was marvelous, the entire royal treasure, consisting of various metals, should suddenly become worthless. And so from that time on accursed envy has deprived mortals of this convenience, as it once deprived them of Eden. For since the jealously of the artisan made him unwilling to teach anyone his secret, the envy of the king was able to destroy the artisan along with his art.[1]

Moved, then, by a divinely inspired charity, I have made available not only to you, but to as many others as possible, and as quickly and carefully as I could, a favor divinely bestowed on me, the most unworthy of men; so that those who come after us, when they learn with the greatest ease the ecclesiastical melodies which I and all my predecessors learned only with the greatest difficulty, will desire my eternal salvation as well as yours and that of my other helpers, and so that our sins will be remitted through God's mercy, or at least that some prayer for our souls will result from the gratitude of so many.

For if at present those who have succeeded in gaining only an imperfect knowledge of singing in ten years of study intercede most devoutly before God for their teachers, what do you think will be done for us and our helpers, who can produce a perfect singer in the space of one year, or at the most in two? And even if such benefits meet with ingratitude from the customary miserliness of mankind, will not a just God reward our labors? Or, since this is God's work and we can do nothing without him, shall we have no reward? Forbid the thought. For even the Apostle, though whatever is done is done by God's grace, sings none the less: "I have fought a good fight, I have finished my course, I have kept the faith. Henceforth there is laid up for me a crown of righteousness."[2]

Confident therefore in our hope of reward, we set about a task of such usefulness; and since after many storms the long-desired fair weather has returned, we must felicitously set sail.

But since you in your captivity are distrustful of liberty, I will set forth the situation in full. John, holder of the most high apostolic seat and now governing the Roman Church,[3] heard of the fame of our school, and because he was greatly curious as to how boys could, by means of our antiphoner, learn songs which they had never heard, he invited me through three emissaries to come to him. I therefore went to Rome with Dom Grunwald, the most reverend abbot, and Dom Peter, provost of the canons of the church of Arezzo, a most learned man by the standards of our time. The Pope was greatly pleased by my arrival, conversing much with me and inquiring of many matters. After repeatedly looking through our antiphoner as if it were some prodigy, and reflecting

---

1. See Petronius, *Satires* 51; there are variants of the story in Pliny, *Natural History* 36.26, and Dio Cassius, *Roman History* 57.21.
2. 2 Timothy 4:7–8.
3. John XIX, pope from 1024 to 1033.

on the rules prefixed to it, he did not give up or leave the place where he sat until he had satisfied his desire to learn a verse himself without having heard it beforehand, thus quickly finding true in his own case what he could hardly believe of others.

Need I say more? I was prevented by illness from remaining in Rome even a short time longer, as the summer heat in the marshy areas near the sea was threatening our demise. We finally came to the agreement that I should return later, at the beginning of winter, and at that time reveal this work of mine more fully to the Pope and his clergy, who had enjoyed a foretaste of it.

A few days after this, desiring to see our spiritual father Dom Guido, Abbot of Pomposa, a man beloved of God and men by the merit of his virtue and wisdom, and a dear friend as well, I paid him a visit. As soon as this man of penetrating intelligence saw our antiphoner, he tested it and found it credible. He regretted that he had once given countenance to our rivals and asked me to come to Pomposa, urging upon me, a monk, that monasteries were to be preferred to bishops' residences, especially Pomposa, because of its zeal for learning, which now by the grace of God and the industry of the most reverend Guido ranks foremost in Italy.

Swayed by the entreaties of so eminent a father, and obeying his instructions, I wish first with God's help to confer distinction upon so notable a monastery by this work and further to reveal myself to the monks as a monk. Since nearly all the bishops have been convicted of simony, I should fear to enter into relations with any of their number.

But since I cannot come to you at present, I am in the meantime addressing to you an excellent method of finding an unknown melody, recently given to us by God and found most useful in practice. Further, I greet especially our foremost helper Dom Martin, the prior of the holy congregation, and with the most earnest entreaties commend my miserable self to his prayers. I also remind Brother Peter, who nourished once by our milk now feeds on the coarsest barley, and who after bowls of golden wine now drinks a mixture of vinegar, to think of one who thinks of him.

To find an unknown melody, most blessed brother, the older and more common procedure is this.[4] You sound on the monochord the letters belonging to each neume, and by listening you will be able to learn the melody as if from hearing it sung by a teacher. But this procedure is childish, good indeed for beginners, but very bad for pupils who have made some progress. For I have seen many keen-witted philosophers who had sought out not merely Italian, but French, German, and even Greek teachers for the study of this art, but who, because they relied on this procedure alone, could never become, I will not say skilled musicians, but even choristers, nor could they duplicate the performance of our choirboys.

---

4. An apparent reference to the method recommended above in the *Dialogue on music* 1 of Pseudo-Odo of Cluny, pp. 90–92.

We do not need to have constant recourse to the voice of a singer or to the sound of some instrument to become acquainted with an unknown melody, so that as if blind we should seem never to go forward without a leader; we need to implant deeply in memory the different qualities of the individual sounds and of all their descents and ascents. You will then have an altogether easy and thoroughly tested method of finding an unknown melody, provided there is someone present to teach the pupil, not merely from a written textbook, but rather by our practice of informal discussion. After I began teaching this procedure to boys, some of them were able before the third day to sing an unknown melody with ease, which by other methods would not have been possible in many weeks.

If, therefore, you wish to commit any note or neume to memory so that it will promptly recur to you whenever you wish in any known or unknown chant, and so that you will be able to sound it at once and with full confidence, you must concentrate upon that note or neume at the beginning of some especially familiar melody. And to retain in your memory any note, you must have at ready command a melody of this description which begins with that note. For example, let it be this melody, which, in teaching boys, I use from beginning to end:

C D F DE D	D D C D E E
Ut que-ant la-xis	Re-so-na-re fi-bris

EEG E D EC D	F G a G FEDD
Mi-- ra ge-sto-rum	Fa-mu-li tu-o---rum,

GaG FE F G D	a G a F Ga a GF ED C E D
Sol- ve pol-lu-ti	La-bi-i re-a--tum, san-cte Jo-an-nes.[5]

Do you not see how the six phrases each begin with a different note? If you, trained as I have described, know the beginning of each phrase so that you can begin any one you wish without hesitation, you will be able to sing these six notes in their proper qualities whenever you see them. Then, when you hear any neume that has not been written down, consider carefully which of these phrases is best adapted to the last note of the neume, so that this last note and the first note of your phrase are of the same pitch. And be sure that the neume ends on the note with which the phrase corresponding to it begins. And when you begin to sing an unknown melody that has been written down, take great care to end each neume so correctly that its last note joins well with the beginning of the phrase which begins with the note on which the neume ends. This rule will be of great use to you either in the competent singing of an unknown

---

5. This hymn melody is not in the earlier hymn collections; its unidiomatic character leads one to assume that it was composed by Guido in order to demonstrate his method.

melody as soon as you see it written down, or in the accurate transcription of an unwritten melody immediately upon hearing it.

I afterwards adapted short fragments of melody to the six notes in sequence. If you examine these phrases closely, you will be pleased to find at the beginning of them all the ascending and descending progressions of each note in turn. If you succeed in singing at will the phrases of each and every one of these fragments, you will have learned by means of a brief and easy rule the exceedingly difficult and manifold varieties of all the neumes. All these matters, which we can hardly explain in writing, we can easily lay bare by a simple discussion.

•   •   •   •   •

The few words on the form of the modes and neumes, which I have set down both in prose and in verse as a prologue to the antiphoner, will briefly and perhaps adequately open the portals to the art of music. And let the painstaking seek out our little book called the *Micrologus*[6] and also read the book *Enchiridion*,[7] composed with great clarity by the most reverend Abbot Odo. I have departed from his example only in the forms of the notes, since I have made concessions to the young, in this not following Boethius, whose treatise is useful to philosophers but not to singers.

6. For a translation of the *Micrologus*, see Claude V. Palisca, ed., *Hucbald, Guido, and John on Music* (New Haven: Yale University Press, 1978), pp. 57–83.
7. That is the *Dialogue on Music* of Pseudo-Odo of Cluny, this volume, pp. 88–100.

21 Anonymous (13th Century)

The *Discantus positio vulgaris,* originating about 1230, contains the earliest surviving description of modal rhythm, the first rhythmic system employed in Western polyphonic music. The short tract appears to be not so much an anonyomous treatise as a compilation of generally accepted doctrine, transmitted by oral tradition. It is preserved in the later-thirteenth-century *Tractatus de musica* of the Dominican friar Jerome of Moravia, where it stands as the first in a series of "positions" on mensural music. It was Jerome, apparently, who assigned it its title, which might be translated "the common or basic position on discant."

Discantus positio vulgaris

After understanding what discant is, it is necessary to look into certain pre-liminary considerations.[1] Now discant is a song that utilizes differing harmonious sounds; and one must know also what an interval *(sonus)* is and how many intervals there are, what is measurable and what is beyond measure, what a ligature is and how it ought to be performed, and what consonance is and what dissonance.

An interval is the occurence of two or more pitches at the same point or at differing points. There are nine intervals, namely, the unison, the semitone, the tone, etc.

That is measurable which is measured by one or more *tempora*.[2] That is beyond measure which is measured by less than one tempus or more than two, like semibreves which are written like this: ♦ ♦ ♦, and a long followed by a long, which has three tempora, like this: ▐ ▐ ▐.

A ligature is the binding together of several linked notes of differing pitch. Groups of two, three, and four notes are bound together according to the following rules.

When two notes are bound in discant, the first is a breve and the second a long, unless the first is written larger than the second, like this: ◼◢. When three are bound, and preceded by a rest, the first is a long, the second a breve, and the third a long; but if preceded by a long, the first two are breves and the third a long; and when followed by a long, the third is longer than a long.[3] If four notes are bound, all are breves. If there are more than four, they do not follow precise rules, but are performed as one pleases, a practice that is particularly appropriate to organum and conductus.

A consonance is the concord of different voice parts on the same pitch or on different pitches. Among concords three are better than others: the unison,

---

TEXT: Simon M. Cserba, ed., *Hieronymus de Moravia O.P. Tractatus de Musica* (Regensburg: Friedrich Pustet, 1935), pp. 189–94. Translation by James McKinnon.

1. On the problematic nature of this opening sentence, see Janet Knapp, "Two Thirteenth-Century Treatises on Modal Rhythm and Discant," *Journal of Music Theory* 6 (1962): p. 214; and Sandra Pinegar, "Textual and Conceptual Relationships among Theoretical Writings on Measurable Music of the Thirteenth and Early Fourteenth Centuries" (Ph.D. diss., Columbia University, 1991), p. 52.

   The present translation was compared with that in the Knapp article and has benefited from that scholar's expertise. Numerous points of chronology and substance involving this reading and those that follow are dependent upon Pinegar's work.

2. At this early point in the history of measured musical duration, a tempus, represented by the breve, is the basic short time value, generally transcribed today by the eighth note. With the gradual addition of shorter note values, the tempus, along with the breve, will come to represent a duration of some length and to have considerable internal division. See, for example, the table below in the reading from Jehan des Murs, p. 157.

3. That is, a long of three tempora, a note beyond measure.

fifth, and octave. The other intervals (modi) are more dissonant than consonant, although this is a matter of degree, with the interval of a single tone seeming to be more dissonant than any other.

It should be noted, moreover, that every note of the plainchant is long beyond measure, containing the measure of three tempora,[4] while every note of the discantus[5] is measurable, either a proper breve or a proper long.[6] Whence it follows that over any note of the cantus firmus at least two notes should be sung, a long and a breve, or something of equal value, like four breves or three with a plica brevis.[7] And the two voice parts should match each other with one of the three consonances mentioned above.

Discant should move up and down in this way: every piece should ascend or descend through one of the nine named intervals, or form a unison.

Let it be known further that all odd notes, when consonant, are more consonant than even notes, and when dissonant, are less dissonant than even notes.[8] Hence, if one ascends or descends from a fifth to a unison, one ought to do so through a third. For example, if the cantus firmus has two successive notes of whatever pitch in unison, say lower F, and the discantus over the first of them is at the fifth, that is upper c, and wishes to descend to the unison at the second note by way of a third, that is upper a, it should so descend, and it should ascend in reverse fashion.[9] If it descends from the octave to the fifth over these same two notes of the same pitch, that is, from upper f to upper c, it should do so by way of the third over the fifth, that is, upper e, and it should ascend from the fifth to the octave in reverse fashion.

If the cantus firmus ascends a semitone, for example, from lower E to lower F, and the discantus is at the octave, upper e, it should descend a major third, through a second,[10] and thus produce a fifth. And when the cantus firmus reverses this process to descend a semitone, then the discantus, now at the fifth, must ascend a major third to produce the octave. If the cantus firmus ascends a tone, from C to D, with the discant at the octave, the discant should

---

4. This refers not to plainchant in general, but to the tenor part of a polyphonic composition which usually employs a segment of chant, the so-called cantus firmus.
5. While discantus is translated "discant" here when referring to the polyphonic genre as a whole, it is translated "discantus" when referring to the upper of the two polyphonic voices.
6. That is, a breve of one tempus and a long of two.
7. One would think three breves rather than four, or two with a plica brevis (a plica or nota plicata—literally a "folded note"—is one drawn with a tail that indicates the singing of a note in addition to the basic one, usually a passing tone to the following note).
8. This means that "odd notes," that is, the first, third, etc., notes of a first mode pattern should be more consonant than the second, fourth, etc., notes. In the examples of discant treatment that follow, the first interval, a perfect consonance, will generally pass to the third interval, another perfect consonance, by way of a lesser consonance.
9. Throughout this entire section that deals with discant treatment, the language is elliptical, omitting especially details of the reverse progressions. A minimum of such details is supplied in what follows.
10. "Through a second"; the text has per secundam a dupla.

descend a minor third by way of a second; and it should ascend in converse fashion when the cantus firmus descends a tone.

If the cantus ascends a minor third, the discantus should descend a tone, and ascend a tone when the discantus descends a minor third. If the cantus ascends a major third, the discantus should descend a semitone; and when the cantus returns by a major third, the discantus ascends a semitone.

If the cantus ascends a fourth, the discantus remains on the same note; and does the same when the cantus descends a fourth. If the cantus firmus ascends a fifth, the discantus moves from its interval of an octave to a fifth by either ascending a tone or descending an octave; and when the cantus firmus descends in return, the discantus ascends an octave.

If the cantus ascends a minor sixth, then the discantus ascends a minor third by way of a second or descends a duplex fourth;[11] and when the cantus descends a minor sixth, then the discantus descends a minor third or ascends a duplex fourth. If the cantus ascends a major sixth, the discantus ascends a major third by way of a second or descends a duplex fourth; and when the cantus returns by descending the like amount, then the discantus descends a major third or ascends a duplex fourth.

If the cantus ascends a duplex fourth, then the discantus descends a major sixth; and when the discantus ascends in reverse, so does the cantus descend. If the cantus ascends an octave, the discantus descends to the fifth; and it ascends in reverse when the cantus descends.

After all this has been observed and committed to memory one can come to possess the entire art of discant by putting it into practice.

One kind of discant is discant proper and another is organum, itself a twofold genre, comprising organum duplex and what is called pure organum. Other kinds of discantus include conductus, motet, and hocket.

Discant proper is a consonant song with different notes but the same text in each voice, as when some ecclesiastical chant is harmonized at the fifth, octave, and twelfth. Duplex organum has the same text but differing notes, with the notes of the tenor long and drawn out, while in the discantus there is a second consonant song differing from the first. Pure organum is that in which two notes of the discant, a long and a breve or something of equal value, correspond to each note beyond measure of the cantus firmus, as described above. Conductus is a consonant polyphonic song using a single poetic text; it employs imperfect consonances.

The motet is a consonant polyphonic song based on the predetermined notes of the cantus firmus, which are either measured or beyond measure; the motet has both diverse notes in each voice and diverse texts. The motet voice utilizes six rhythmic modes: the first consists of a long followed by a breve, the second of a breve followed by a long; the third of a long and two breves; the fourth of

---

11. This is true only if one takes the duplex fourth to mean a perfect fourth and a tritone; see the next situation where in fact two perfect fourths is the correct interval.

two breves and a long; the fifth entirely of longs; and the sixth entirely of breves and semibreves. The following rules govern their relationship to the tenor.

To begin with the first mode: at times the tenor corresponds to the motetus, as in *Virgo decus castitatis*,[12] so that every long of the motetus matches a long of the tenor, and similarly every breve matches a breve. A rest in either voice has the value of one breve, unless both voices pause together with the triplum,[13] and then the rests in the cantus firmus are held ad libitum. Sometimes the tenor consists entirely of longs, as does the tenor of the motet *O Maria maris stella,* and then a long and a breve of the motetus will always correspond to a long of the tenor.[14] The rest in each voice here is long, unless both pause together with the triplum, a situation treated as described previously.

In the second mode as well, the tenor sometimes corresponds to the notes of the motetus, as they do to some extent in *In omni fratre tuo sum* and in *Gaude chorus omnium.* Sometimes there is no such correspondence and the tenor consists entirely of longs; in that case everything is the opposite of the first mode. The rests of each voice also correspond.

Similarly in the third mode, when the tenor corresponds to the motetus, as in *O natio nephandi generis*, every long of the motetus matches every long of the tenor, and every breve matches every breve. But when the tenor consists entirely of long notes, as in *O Maria beata genitrix*, one long of the tenor has the same value as one long of the motetus, followed by a long of the tenor matching two breves of the motetus.[15] The rests of each ought to have this same value, unless both voices pause together with the triplum, and then they are as described before. In the fourth mode, whether the motetus corresponds to the tenor or not, everything maintains the opposite of the third mode, including the rests.

As for the fifth and sixth modes, whether their motetus parts match their tenors or not, it can be gathered from what has been said already how they must conform to the tenors at rests and even to the tripla of other modes.

A hocket is a concordant polyphonic song composed over a tenor, in one of the modes of the motets, but lacking words.[16]

---

12. See Knapp for manuscript references to the motets cited here.
13. The triplum (*tripla* here) is a third voice, added above the motetus.
14. Here the text adds the inexplicable phrase *et e converso* (and vice versa).
15. The sentence concludes with another confusing *et e converso.*
16. A hocket is a composition, or more often a passage within a composition, in which the melodic line is given in rapid distribution between two voice parts, so that when one sounds the other observes a rest. The term hocket is onomatopoetic, related etymologically to a variety of similar words, including the English language hiccup.

22 Johannes de Garlandia

Jerome of Moravia ended his transcription of the *Discantus positio vulgaris* with the following comment. "This is the first position. Since certain of the Nations [i.e., national student groups of thirteenth-century Paris] use it in common, and since it is older than the others, we refer to it as common *(vulgaris)*. But because it is defective, we follow it with the position of Johannes de Garlandia." It is particularly defective, at least from the modern pedagogical point of view, in that it fails to explain how the six rhythmic modes are expressed in notation; and therefore the relevant chapter from the treatise attributed to Johannes is provided here.

The identity of this Johannes remains problematic (see Pinegar, "Textual and Conceptual Relationships," 78–102.) Among the factors complicating the question are the circumstances that the content of the treatise reflects musical practice from the first half of the century, and the existence of at least two figures named Johannes de Garlandia, one a poet and the other a music theorist, both of whom were late thirteenth-century figures. Perhaps the music theorist in question brought the treatise to Jerome's attention and was thus credited with its composition.

FROM *De musica mensurabili*

4. THE DEMONSTRATION OF THE MODES IN NOTATION

The first rule of the first mode calls for three notes in ligature at the beginning followed by two in ligature, and two more, etc., indefinitely. All ligatures must have both propriety and perfection:[1]

Angelus.

TEXT: Erich Reimer, ed., *Johannes de Garlandia: De mensurabili musica*, Beihefte zum Archiv für Musikwissenschaft 10 (Wiesbaden: Franz Steiner, 1972), pp. 52–56. Translation by James McKinnon.

1. Propriety and perfection refer to the customary ways of writing the beginning and ending, respectively, of ligatures; see Franco of Cologne below for a full explanation and illustration.

A second rule of the first mode: three notes in ligature with a breve rest, etc., indefinitely. One can understand it as given here:

Angelus.

Angelus

The first rule of the second mode calls for two notes in ligature with propriety,[2] followed by two, etc., with three in ligature at the end without propriety and with perfection:

Balaam.

Balaam

A second rule of the same mode: a three-note ligature without propriety and with perfection followed by a long rest, a pattern repeated indefinitely as given here:

Balaam.

Balaam

The third mode is notated with an initial long note followed by a series of three-note ligatures with propriety:

---

2. It can be assumed here, and in each similar instance that follows, that a ligature described simply as "with propriety" is also to have perfection.

Cumque.

Cumque

The fourth mode is expressed by a series of three-note ligatures with propriety, concluded by a two-note ligature without perfection and a long rest:

Docebit.

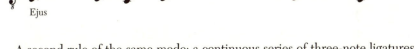

Docebit

The fifth mode is expressed exclusively by long notes:

Eius.

Ejus

A second rule of the same mode: a continuous series of three-note ligatures with propriety and perfection, followed by a long rest. This is done for the sake of brevity and is not expressed properly; but it is used because it is accepted as such in the tenors of motets:

Et sperabit.

Et sperabit

The sixth mode is expressed in this way: a four-note ligature with propriety and plica, followed by a series of two-note ligatures with plica:

A second rule of the same mode: it is not justified by this discipline, but it can be demonstrated by an example that one finds in the triplum of the Alleluia *Posui adjutorium,* namely, a four-note ligature with propriety, followed by a series of three-note ligatures with propriety, as given in the above-mentioned Alleluia:

23 Franco of Cologne

Although Franco of Cologne is a central figure in the history of European music theory, little is known for certain about his life. A fourteenth-century manuscript concludes the *Ars cantus mensurabilis* (The Art of Mensurable Music) by attributing it to "Franco, papal chaplain and preceptor of the Cologne Commandery of the Hospital of St. John of Jerusalem." Jacques of Liège, moreover, confirms Franco's German origins by calling him *Franco Teutonicus.* That Franco had moved to Paris where he was active in musical circles is strongly suggested by references to him in the writings of theorists with Parisian ties; in addition to the later Jacques of Liège there is the nearly contemporary Anonymous IV, who credits Franco with important rhythmic innovations. A fifteenth-century manuscript calls him "Magister Franco of Paris," pointing to a connection with the University of Paris.

The central innovation of his treatise, and one of the most fundamentally important in the history of Western notation, is the movement away from defining the rhythmic value of musical notes by their context—as in earlier modal notation—toward assigning fixed values to individual notes. It is true that a measure of relativity remains in his system; he defines all rhythmic values within the context of the so-called perfection, a unit of three short notes, but the break with the earlier thirteenth century is nonetheless decisive and irreversible. Recent scholarship tends to place the date of the *Ars cantus mensurabilis* quite late, about 1280, which might seem to detract from the originality of a work that summarizes mid-century musical practice. But the same scholarship confirms that Franco's treatise, whatever its date, is the first clear and coherent exposition of the principles underlying that practice.

Ars cantus mensurabilis

PROLOGUE

Now that the philosophers have treated sufficiently of plainsong and have fully explained it to us both theoretically and practically (theoretically above all Boethius, practically Guido Monachus, and, as to the ecclesiastical tropes, especially the blessed Gregory); we propose—in accordance with the entreaties of certain influential persons and without losing sight of the natural order—to treat of mensurable music, which plainsong, described so well by the philosophers cited above, precedes as does the principal the subaltern.

Let no one say that we began this work out of arrogance or merely for our own convenience; we began it rather out of evident necessity, for the ready apprehension of our readers, and the thorough instruction of all copiers of mensurable music. For when we see many, both moderns and ancients, saying sound things about mensurable music in their treatises on the arts but being on the other hand deficient and erroneous in many respects, especially in the details of the science, we think their views are to be supplemented, lest perchance as a result of their deficiency and error the science be exposed to harm.

We therefore propose to expound mensurable music in a compendium, in which we shall not hesitate to introduce things well said by others or to disprove and avoid their errors and, if we have discovered some new thing, to uphold and prove it with good reasons.

1. OF THE DEFINITION OF MENSURABLE MUSIC AND ITS SPECIES

Mensurable music is song measured by long and short units of time. To understand this definition, let us consider what measure is and what time is.

TEXT: Gilbert Reaney and André Gilles, eds., *Franconis de Colonia Ars Cantus Mensurabilis*, Corpus Scriptorum de Musica, no. 18 (Rome, 1974). Translation by Oliver Strunk, revised by James McKinnon.

Measure is an quantitative attribute showing the length and brevity of any mensurable melody. I say mensurable, because in plainsong this kind of measure is not present. Time is the measure of a sound's duration as well as of the opposite, the omission of a sound, commonly called a rest. I say rest is measured by time, because if this were not the case two different melodies—one with rests, the other without—could not be proportionately accommodated to one another.

Mensurable music is divided into wholly and partly mensurable. Music wholly mensurable is discant, because discant is measured by time in all its voice parts. Music partly mensurable is organum, because organum is not measured in all its voice parts. The word organum, be it known, is used in two senses—in its proper sense and in the sense commonly accepted. For organum in its proper sense is organum duplum, also called organum purum. But in the sense commonly accepted, organum is any ecclesiastical chant measured by time.

Since the simple precedes the complex, let us speak first of discant.

2. OF THE DEFINITION AND DIVISION OF DISCANT

Discant is a consonant combination of different melodies proportionately accommodated to one another by long, short, or still shorter sounds and expressed in writing as mutually proportioned by suitable figures. Discant is divided in this way: one kind is sounded simply; another, called hocket, is disconnected; another, called copula, is connected. Of these we must speak in turn, but since every discant proceeds by mode let us explain first about the modes and afterwards about their signs and figures.

3. OF THE MODES OF EVERY DISCANT

Mode is the knowledge of sound measured by long and short intervals of time. Different authorities count the modes and place them in order differently, some allowing six, others seven. We, however, allow only five, since to these five all others may be reduced.[1]

The first mode proceeds entirely by longs. With it we combine the one which proceeds by a long and a breve—for two reasons: first, because the same rests are common to both; second, to put a stop to the controversy between the ancients and some of the moderns. The second mode proceeds by a breve and a long, the third by a long and two breves, the fourth by two breves and a long, the fifth entirely by breves and semibreves.

1. Here Franco departs from the more familiar categorization of six modes as, for example, that seen above in both the *Discantus positio vulgaris* and in Johannes de Garlandia, 4, pp. 113–116. He does so by combining the first and fifth modes into one, with the first mode in the upper voice and the fifth in the tenor. See Pinegar, "Textual and Conceptual Relationships among Theoretical Writings on Measurable Music of the Thirteenth and Early Fourteenth Centuries," pp. 392–447, for a thorough discussion of the various thirteenth-century categorizations.

But since sounds are the cause and principle of the modes, and notes are the signs of sounds, it is obvious that we ought to explain about notes, or about figures, which are the same. And since discant itself is governed both by actual sound and by the opposite, that is, by its omission,[2] and since these two things are different, their signs will also be different because different objects require different signs. And since actual sound precedes its omission, just as "habit" precedes "privation,"[3] let us speak of figures, which represent actual sound, before speaking of rests, which represent its omission.

4. OF THE FIGURES OR SIGNS OF MENSURABLE MUSIC

A figure is a representation of a sound arranged in one of the modes. From this it follows that the figures ought to indicate the modes and not, as some have maintained, the contrary. Figures are either simple or composite. The composite figures are the ligatures. Of simple figures there are three species: long, breve, and semibreve, the first of which has three varieties—perfect, imperfect, and duplex.

The perfect long is said to be the first and principal, for in it all the others are included and all the others are reducible to it. It is called perfect because it is measured by three tempora, the ternary number being the most perfect number because it takes its name from the Holy Trinity, which is true and pure perfection. Its figure is quadrangular, with a descending tail on the right that represents length: ▍.

The imperfect long has the same figure as the perfect, but signifies only two tempora. It is called imperfect because it is never found except in combination with a preceding or following breve. From this it follows that those who call it proper *(recta)* are in error, for that which is proper can stand by itself.

The duplex long, formed in this way ▄▌, signifies two longs that are combined in one figure so that the line of plainsong in the tenor need not be broken up.

The breve, although it has two varieties, proper and altered, is represented in each case by a quadrangular figure without a tail: ■ .

Of the semibreve one variety is major, the other minor, although both are represented by the same lozenge-shaped figure: ◆ .

5. OF THE MUTUAL ARRANGEMENT OF FIGURES

The valuation of simple figures is dependent on their arrangement with respect to one another. This arrangement is understood, moreover, in that after a long there follows either a long or a breve. And let it be observed that the same is true of the valuation of breves and semibreves.

---

2. *Vox recta* is translated "actual sound" here and *vox amissa*, "its omission"; see Johannes de Garlandia 1.
3. For the philosophical terms "habit" and "privation" see Richard McKeon, *Selections from Medieval Philosophers*, vol. 2 (New York, Scribner's, 1930), Glossary.

If a long follows a long, then the first long, whether it be a figure or a rest, is measured under one accent by three tempora and called a perfect long:

But if a breve follows a long, the case is manifold, for there will be either a single breve or several of them.

If a single breve, then the long is of two tempora and called imperfect:

unless there be placed between the two, namely between the long and the breve, that little stroke that is called the "sign of perfection" by some and the "division of the mode" by others. In this case, the first long is perfect, and the breve makes the following long imperfect:

If several breves, the case is again manifold, for there might be two, three, four, five, or more than five.

If only two:

then then the long is perfect unless a single breve precedes it:

Of the two breves, the first, moreover, is called a breve proper, the second an altered breve. (A breve proper is one which contains one tempus only. An altered breve, while the same as the imperfect long in value, differs from it in form, for both, though differently figured, are measured by two tempora. What we call a tempus is the minimum duration to be sung in fullness of voice.) But if the stroke called division of the mode is placed between the aforesaid two breves:

then the first long is imperfect and the second also, while the breves will both be proper. This, however, is most unusual.

If only three breves stand between the two longs:

the case is the same as before, except that the one which we called altered breve in the first instance is here divided into two breves proper. But if between the first breve and the two following ones there is placed a division of the mode:

then the first long is made imperfect by the first breve, and of the two following breves the first becomes a breve proper while the last is altered. Observe also that three tempora, whether under one accent or under several, constitute a perfection.

If more than three breves:

then the first long is always imperfect unless the sign of perfection is added to it:

Of the following breves, all are proper that are found in counting by that ternary number which creates a perfection. But if at the end only two remain, the second is an altered breve:

while if only one remains, it will be proper and will make the final long imperfect:

The valuation of semibreves and breves is the same as in the rules already given. But observe that there cannot stand for a breve proper more than three semibreves (called minor semibreves, since they are the smallest parts of the breve proper):

or less than two (of which the first is called a minor semibreve, the second a major, since it includes in itself two minor ones):

But if three semibreves follow immediately after two standing for a breve proper, or vice versa:

then let a division of the mode be placed between three and two, or vice versa, as shown in the preceding example. For an altered breve, moreover, there cannot stand less than four semibreves:

or more than six:

for the altered breve includes within itself two breves proper. From this appears the mendacity of those who at one time replace the altered breve with three semibreves and at other times with two.

6. OF PLICAS IN SIMPLE FIGURES

Aside from these there are certain other simple figures, indicating the same things and called by the same names, but with the addition of what we call the plica.[4] Let us then consider what the plica is; it is a note dividing the same sound into low and high. Plicas are long, breve, and semibreve. But for the present we shall say nothing about the semibreve plica, for it cannot occur in simple figures, although, as will appear later on, it may be used in ligatures and groups of semibreves.

Plicas, further, are either ascending or descending. The long ascending plica is a quadrangular figure bearing on the right a single ascending stroke: ◼ or, more properly, bearing two strokes of which the right one is longer than the left: ◼. I say more properly, for it is from these two strokes that the plica takes its name. The long descending plica likewise has two strokes, but descending ones with the right stroke longer than the left, as before: ◥.

The breve ascending plica is that which has two ascending strokes, the left one, however, longer than the right: ◼. The descending breve plica has two descending strokes with the longer one on the left: ◤.

Observe also that these plicas have a force similar to that of the simple figures already mentioned and that they are similarly regulated as to value.

7. OF LIGATURES AND THEIR PROPERTIES

Now that simple figures have been discussed, let us speak about those that are composite or, what amounts to the same thing, bound together, those that are rightly called ligatures.

A ligature is a combination of simple figures arranged by the proper strokes of the pen. Ligatures are either ascending or descending. In an ascending ligature the second note is higher than the first; in a descending ligature the first note is higher than the second. Ligatures, moreover, are said to be "with propriety," "without propriety," or "with opposite propriety." And this is with respect to the beginning of the ligature. With respect to the end, however, they are said to be either "with perfection" or "without perfection."

Observe also that these differences are essential and specific to the ligature themselves. Hence a ligature with propriety differs essentially from one that is without, just as a rational being differs from an irrational one, and the same is true of the other differences we have mentioned. Species is subordinate to genus. Yet to the species themselves no name is given, but the differences we have mentioned and the genus to which they belong define them. This agrees

4. *Plica*, a fold, from *plicare*, to fold or double up.

with what occurs in other real genera: "animate body," for example, defines a certain species to which no name is given.

With respect to the middle notes of ligatures no essential difference is found, from which it follows that all the middle notes of a ligature agree in significance. Hence it appears that the position of those is false who hold that in one type of ternary ligature the middle note is a long,[5] even though it is a breve in all the others.

Now let us consider what is meant by with propriety, without propriety, and with opposite propriety, also by with perfection and without perfection, and what the significance of all these may be. Propriety applies to the first note of a ligature that retains its original form derived from plainsong; perfection means the same thing, but with respect to the final note. Whence follow the rules of the differences we have mentioned.

Every descending ligature having a stroke descending from the left side of the first note is called with propriety, being so figured in plainsong. If it lacks the stroke it is without propriety. Further, every ascending ligature is with propriety if it lacks the stroke. If, however, it has a stroke descending from the left side of the first note, or from the right side, which is more proper, it is without propriety.

Further, every ligature, whether ascending or descending, that has a stroke ascending from the first note, is with opposite propriety.

Now with respect to the final note of a ligature the following rules are given. Every ligature that has the final note immediately above the penultimate is perfect. A ligature is made imperfect in two ways: first, if the final note be rectangular, without a plica, the head turned away from (instead of being above) the penultimate; second, if the last two notes be combined in one ascending oblique form, or descending oblique form. In ascent, however, this last imperfection is out of use, nor is it necessary except, as will appear later on, when the final breve in an ascending ligature is to take a plica.

And let it be known that, just as one ligature differs from another in form by way of these differences, so also does it differ in value. Whence follow the rules of all ligatures. In every ligature with propriety the first note is a breve, in every one without propriety, a long. In every ligature with perfection the final note is a long, in every one without perfection, a breve. In every ligature with opposite propriety the first note is a semibreve, to which we add, and the following one, not in itself, but in consequence, for no semibreve may occur alone. Further, every middle note is a breve, except, as already explained, it be made a semibreve by opposite propriety. Be it also understood that in ligatures the longs are made perfect in the way that was explained under simple figures and that the breves in a similar way become proper or are altered.

---

5. See Johannes de Garlandia, 4, pp. 114–15, where his alternate forms of the second and fifth modes call for a long in the middle of a three-note ligature.

8. OF PLICAS IN COMPOSITE FIGURES

Aside from this let it be known that any ligature, whether perfect or imperfect, may take the plica, and this with respect to its end. (What a plica is, has already been explained under simple figures.) For perfect ligatures may take the plica in two ways, ascending or descending. Imperfect ligatures may also take the plica in two ways. And observe that imperfect ligatures always take the plica in oblique imperfection, ascending or descending. And in such a case, where an imperfect ligature is to take a plica, the oblique form must be used in ascending, because the final note is to be made a breve. For if the rectangular imperfection takes the plica, the plica will make it perfect, since it shares the rule of perfection.[6] Without the plica, the oblique imperfection is not to be used, for the rectangular form of imperfection suffices wherever there is no plica and is more proper and more usual. Thus are the plicas of all ligatures made clear.

There are also certain combinations of simple figures and ligatures which share the nature, in part of ligatures, in part of simple figures, and which cannot be called either the one or the other.[7] For the valuation of such combinations we can give no rules other than those already given for simple figures and ligatures. Besides, there are other arrangements of simple figures and ligatures, distinguished by the rules of simple figures alone, which supply the defect of the combinations not governed by rule.

9. OF RESTS AND OF HOW THROUGH THEIR AGENCY THE MODES ARE CHANGED FROM ONE TO ANOTHER

The signs signifying actual sound having been discussed, let us consider the rests, which represent its omission. A rest is an omission of actual sound in the quantity proper to some mode. Of rests there are six species: perfect long, imperfect long (under which is included the altered breve, since they both involve the same duration), breve proper, major semibreve, minor semibreve, and the double bar (*finis punctorum*).

The rest of a perfect long is the omission of a perfect actual sound, comprehending in itself three tempora. The rest of an imperfect long and altered breve is measured in a similar way by two tempora only. The rest of a breve is the omission of a breve proper, including in itself a single tempus. The major semibreve omits two parts of the breve proper, the minor a third part only. The double bar is called immensurable, for it occurs also in plainsong. This signifies simply that regardless of the mode the penultimate note is a long, even though it would be a breve if the mode were considered.

6. That is, the plica will give it the appearance of a long because it is to the right of the note as in the long plica.
7. Franco refers here to the so-called *conjuncturae*, notational combinations derived from the climacus and similar neumes of plain chant, which appeared to the theorists of his time to have mensural significance.

Further, these six rests are designated by six fine strokes, themselves referred to as rests. Of these the first, called perfect, touching four lines, covers three spaces, since it is measured by three tempora. For the same reason the imperfect rest, touching three lines, covers two spaces, the breve rest one space, the major semibreve rest two parts of one space, the minor semibreve rest one part only. The double bar, touching all lines, covers four spaces.

The forms for all these are shown in the following example:

Observe also that rests have a marvelous power, for through their agency the modes are transformed from one to another. The proper rest of the first mode is the breve proper or perfect long; that of the second the imperfect long; the proper rests of the third and fourth are perfect longs, though, improperly, proper or altered breves; the fifth ought properly to have the breve or semibreve rest. Now if the first mode, which proceeds by long, breve, and long, has an imperfect long rest after a breve:

it is changed to the second. If the second mode has a breve rest after a long:

it is changed to the first.

The fifth mode, when combined with the first in any discant, is governed by the rests of the first and has a long note before a rest:

When combined with the second, it is governed by the rests of the second and has a breve at the end before the rest:

When it is neither the one nor the other, it is governed by its own rests:

Observe also that all the modes may run together in a single discant, for through perfections all are reduced to one. Nor need one attempt to determine the mode to which such a discant belongs, although it may be said to belong to the one in which it chiefly or frequently remains.

Let this be enough for the present of rests and of the changing of the modes.

10. HOW MANY FIGURES CAN BE BOUND AT ONE TIME?

Be it known that not to bind a figure that can be bound is a fault, but to bind a figure that cannot be bound a greater fault. Whence be it observed that longs cannot be bound together except in the binary ligature that is without propriety and with perfection. Nor is it a fault if even in this situation they are not bound, for nowhere else are longs bound together. From this it follows that those who occasionally bind three longs together, as in tenors, err exceedingly, as do those who bind a long between two breves, since, as we have seen, all middle notes become breves by rule.

Similarly, more than two semibreves cannot be bound together, and then only at the beginning of the ligature, a practice which is reserved to semibreves. Breves can be bound at the beginning, in the middle, and at the end of a ligature.

From these things it is evident that any mode written without words, except the mode which proceeds entirely by longs, can be bound. The first mode, which proceeds by long and breve, first binds three without propriety and with perfection, then two with propriety and perfection, and as many more twos as desired, so that it concludes with two of this species, unless the mode is changed.

Observe also, as already explained in the chapter on rests, that the modes can be changed in several ways. The second mode begins with a binary ligature with propriety and perfection, then two, two, and so forth, of the same species, a single breve remaining at the end, unless the mode is changed.

The third mode begins with a four-note ligature without propriety and with perfection, then three with propriety and perfection, then three, three, and so forth, unless the mode is changed.

The fourth mode first binds three with propriety and perfection, then three, three, and so forth, of the same species, concluding with two with propriety and without perfection, unless the mode is changed.

The fifth mode ought to be bound as far as possible, concluding with breves or semibreves, unless the mode is changed.

11. OF DISCANT AND ITS SPECIES

Now that figures and rests have been considered, let us speak of how discant ought to be made and of its species. But since every discant is governed by consonances, let us first consider the consonances and dissonances that are sounded at the same time and in different voice parts.[8]

By concord we mean two or more pitches so sounded at one time that the ear perceives them to agree with one another. By discord we mean the opposite, namely, two sounds so combined that the ear perceives them to be dissonant.

Of concords there are three species: perfect, imperfect, and intermediate. Concords are perfect when two sounds are so combined that, because of the consonance, one is scarcely perceived to differ from the other. Of these there are two: unison and diapason. Concords are imperfect when the ear perceives that two sounds differ considerably, yet are not discordant. Of these there are two: ditone and semiditone. Concords are intermediate when two sounds are so combined that they produce a concord better than the imperfect, yet not better than the perfect. Of these there are two: diapente and diatessaron. As to why one concord is more concordant than another, let this be left to plainsong.

Of discords there are two species: perfect and imperfect. Discords are perfect when two sounds are so combined that the ear perceives them to disagree with one another. Of these there are four: semitone, tritone, ditone plus diapente, and semitone plus diapente. Discords are imperfect when the ear perceives that two sounds agree with one another to a certain extent, yet are discordant. Of these there are three: tone, tone plus diapente, and semiditone plus diapente.

Observe also that both concords and discords can be endlessly extended, as in diapente plus diapason and diatessaron plus diapason, and similarly by adding the double and triple diapason, if it be possible for the voice. Be it also known that immediately before a concord any imperfect discord concords well.

Discant is written either with words or with and without words. If with words, there are two possibilities—with a single text or with several texts. Discant is written with a single text in the cantilena, in the rondellus, and in any ecclesiastical chant. It is written with several texts in motets which have a

8. Franco's treatment of concord and discord, although differing in some details, is clearly derived from that of Johannes de Garlandia, 9.

triplum and a tenor, for the tenor is the equivalent of some text. It is written with and without words in the conductus and in the ecclesiastical discant improperly called organum.

Observe also that except for the conductus the procedure is the same in all these forms, for in all except the conductus there is first heard some *cantus prius factus* (called tenor, since it supports the discant and has its place on its own). In the conductus, however, this is not the case, for cantus and discant are written by the same person. The term discant, however, is used in two senses—first, as meaning something sung by a number of persons; second, as meaning something based on a chant.

The following procedures are employed in discant. The discant begins either in unison with the tenor:

or at the diapason:

or at the diapente:

or at the diatessaron:

or at the ditone:

or at the semiditone:

proceeding then by concords, sometimes introducing discords in suitable places, so that when the tenor ascends the discant descends, and vice versa. Be it also known that sometimes, to enhance the beauty of a composition, the tenor and discant ascend and descend together:

Be it also understood that in all the modes concords are always to be used at the beginning of a perfection, whether this beginning be a long, a breve, or a semibreve.

In conductus the procedure is different, for he who wishes to write a conductus must first invent as beautiful a melody as he can, then, as previously explained, use it as a tenor is used in writing discant.

He who wishes to construct a triplum must have the tenor and discant in mind, so that if the triplum be discordant with the tenor, it will not be discordant with the discant, and vice versa. And let him proceed further by concords, ascending or descending now with the tenor, now with the discant, so that his triplum is not always with either one alone:

Dulcia

He who wishes to construct a quadruplum or quintuplum ought to have in mind the melodies already written, so that if it be discordant with one, it will be in concord with the others. Nor ought it always to ascend or descend with any one of these, but now with the tenor, now with the discant, and so forth.

Be it observed also that in discant, as also in tripla and so forth, the equivalence in the perfections of longs, breves, and semibreves ought always to be borne in mind, so that there may be as many perfections in the discant, triplum, and so forth, as there are in the tenor, and vice versa, counting both actual sounds and their omissions as far as the penultimate perfection, where such measure is not observed but rather a point of organum.

Let this be enough for the present of simple discant.

12. OF COPULA

A copula is a rapid, connected discant, either bound or unbound. A bound copula is one which begins with a simple long and proceeds by binary ligatures with propriety and perfection as in the second mode, although it differs from the second mode in notation and in performance. It differs in notation, since the second mode does not begin with a simple long as the copula does:

If a division of the mode is placed between the initial long and the following ligature, it is no longer a copula, but is said to be in the second mode:

A -   men

It differs from the second mode also in performance, since the second mode is performed with a proper breve and imperfect long, while the copula is performed quickly, as though with semibreve and breve, right through to the end.

An unbound copula resembles the fifth mode, although it differs from it in two respects—in notation and in performance. It differs in notation, since the fifth mode can be bound wherever there are no words, while the copula, although it is never used with words, is unbound:

In performance it differs also, since the fifth mode is performed with proper breves, while the copula is more quickly connected in performance.

Let this be enough of copula.

13. OF HOCKET

A truncation is a sort of music sounded in a broken way by actual sounds and their omissions. Be it known also that a truncation can be effected in as many ways as the long, breve, and semibreve can be divided. The long is divisible in a number of ways. First, it can be divided into long and breve, or breve and long, and from this division a truncation or hocket (for this is the same thing) is so effected that in one voice a breve is omitted and in the other a long:

(In seculum)

Then it can also be divided into three breves, or two, and into several semibreves, and from all these divisions a truncation is so sung by actual sounds and their omissions that when one voice rests, the other does not, and vice versa.

The breve, on the other hand, can be divided into three semibreves or two, and from this division a hocket is sung by omitting a semibreve in one voice and performing one in the other:

Be it observed that by way of these truncations, the omission and sounding of longs and breves, the vernacular hockets are sung. Be it observed also that in every case the equivalence of the tempora and the concord of the actual sounds must be borne in mind. And let it be known that every truncation must be based on a cantus prius factus, whether it is in the vernacular or Latin.

Let this suffice for hocket.

14. OF ORGANUM[9]

Organum, in the proper sense of the word, is a sort of music not measured in all its parts. Be it known that there can be no organum except over a single sustained note in the tenor, for when the tenor has several notes within a short space, discant is the immediate result:

[Constan - tes   e - sto - te]

The longs and breves of organum are determined by three rules. The first is: whatever is written as a simple long note is long; as a breve, short; as a semibreve, still shorter. The second is: whatever is long requires concord with respect to the tenor; if a long occur as a discord, let the tenor be silent or render itself concordant:[10]

[Ju -   dea]

9. On this chapter, see Charles M. Atkinson, "Franco of Cologne on the Rhythm of Organum Purum," *Early Music History* 9 (1989): 1–26.
10. Thus the second note of the tenor is changed from an F, the original pitch of the chant from which it is derived, to an E in order to form a consonance with the upper voice.

The third is: Whatever occurs immediately before the rest which we call the double bar is long, for every penultimate note is long.

Be it observed also that in organum purum, whenever several figures occur over a sustained note, only the first is to be sung in measure, while all the rest are to observe the florid style.[11]

Of discant and its species, of signs (that is, of figures and rests), and of organum let what has been said here suffice.

Here ends the great "Art of music" of that reverend man, Dominus Franco, papal chaplain and preceptor of the Cologne Commandery of the Hospital of St. John of Jerusalem.

11. The translation of this difficult passage follows the interpretation of Atkinson, pp. 10–23.

24 Aegidius of Zamora

Aegidius was born at Zamora in northwestern Spain about 1240 and entered the Franciscan order in about 1270. He studied in Paris in the early 1270s and then returned to Spain, where he lived the rest of his long life as a scholar and ecclesiastical figure of some prominence. He worked, for example, at the court of Alphonso the Wise, for whom he compiled the celebrated *Cantigas de Santa Maria*. He was Minister of the Santiago province of the Franciscan Order from 1303 to 1318 and died some years later at an unknown date.

Aegidius dedicated his *Ars musica* to Jean Mincio de Murrovalle, Minister General of the Franciscan Order from 1296 to 1304. It is a conservative work that fails to mention polyphony and attempts rather to summarize the views of the traditional authorities on theoretical topics involving plainchant. One of the more original sections, Chapter II (translated here) deals with the exploits of musical animals, an area in which Aegidius, the author of a natural history, had special expertise. Another chapter frequently cited is the final one, in which he discourses at some length on musical instruments; unfortunately it is not known whether this is the work of Aegidius himself or if it was borrowed from Bartholomeus Anglicus.

FROM *Ars Musica*

CHAPTER I: ON THE ORIGINAL DISCOVERY
OF THE MUSICAL ART

We read that, according to the diverse views of many savants, there were numerous discoverers of music. Others, however, have insisted that the philosopher Pythagoras, while passing by a smithy, heard a ringing sound produced by the beating of five hammers upon one anvil. He approached the place, led there by the sweet and melodious concord that arose from the diversity of sound, and carefully considered whether some secret of the musical art might lie hidden in the sound of these hammers. At this very spot, then, he set out immediately to weigh the hammers; one by one he briskly distinguished the various pitches from the ringing of the hammers, and thereby discovered the seven notes of the scale and the consonances.

Yet if we can assume from what has been said that the philosopher Pythagoras discovered something of this art by means of his alert intelligence, he was nevertheless not the very first inventor or founder of the art. As we are informed by the divinely inspired narratives in the Hebraic truth of Genesis, Chapter 4, and from the gloss on that passage, from Rhabanus, from the distinguished historiographer Josephus, and from the *Historia scholastica*,[1] Tubal, son of Lamech by his wife Ada, was the father of those who play upon the cithara and organ—but not the father of the instruments themselves, which were invented long afterwards. This man was the very first to discover the proportions and consonances of music, so that the work of a shepherd, which was so burdensome and debilitating to the body with its sleeplessness, exertions, and anxieties, would be rendered pleasurable. When Tubal heard, then, that Adam had prophesied concerning two judgments, one through water and a second through fire, he meticulously inscribed the science of music upon two pillars, thus transmitting the principles of this art in writing, lest what he had discovered be lost. Now one of these pillars was of marble, which could not be dissolved by the Flood, and the other was of brick, which could not be destroyed by fire. Indeed the marble one, according to Josephus, was later discovered in Syria.[2]

The above-mentioned Lamech fathered Tubalcain by his second wife Sella; Tubalcain was, as Chapter 4 of Genesis relates, a smith in every sort of bronze and ironwork. He was the original founder of the art of metalworking, and he

---

TEXT: Michel Robert-Tissot, ed., *Johannes Aegidius de Zamora: Ars musica*, Corpus Scriptorum de Musica, no. 20 (Rome, 1974), pp. 36–52. Translation by James McKinnon.

1. The *Historia scholastica, Liber Genesis XXVIII*, of Peter Comestor is a particularly important source for Aegidius in what follows.
2. Flavius Josephus, *Antiquitates Judaicae* 2.64.

expertly fashioned the tools of war. He also created sculptures in metal, that is, examples of metalwork that delighted the eye. Now as Tubalcain worked, Tubal (or Jubal), of whom we spoke before, was delighted by the sound of the hammers, as we read in the *Historia scholastica* histories, and he cleverly calculated (as told above) from the weights of the hammers the proportions and the consonances which arise from them. The Greeks falsely attributed this discovery to Pythagoras (again, as told above). Similarly it was in working with shrubbery that Tubalcain discovered how to fashion intriguing works in metal that delight the eye, like the consonances that delight the ear of musicians. For when the brothers had burned the brush in the fields so that the tender grass would sprout for the flocks, veins of metallic ore flowed into rivulets. According to Josephus, after these rivulets had formed into metal sheets and the brothers had lifted them up and supported them, they found the shapes of the places (in which the metal sheets had lain) impressed upon those very sheets.[3]

It should be noted, moreover, that Zoroaster (called Cham by some), the inventor of the magical arts, elegantly inscribed the seven liberal arts on fourteen pillars. Seven of the pillars were of bronze and seven of brick, to resist the Flood and fire mentioned above. But Ninus had his books consigned to the flames whence they perished. Abraham, who excelled in his knowledge of the stars, instructed this Zoroaster in the liberal arts. Still, Isidore states in the fifth book, second chapter, of his *Etymologies* that Tubal, the offspring of Cain, invented music before the Flood. The Greeks, however, according to Isidore, attributed this to Pythagoras, claiming that he discovered it in the sound of hammers and in the striking of stretched strings.[4]

Others, according to Isidore, say that the Theban philosopher Linus, or the philosophers Zethus and Amphion discovered music. After these, continues Isidore, there were further claims from time to time; as the poet would have it, "the new author must always make his own contribution." We read, accordingly, that music was discovered by the philosopher Asclepiadis in the tinkling sound of gold; while some claim it was by some other philosopher from the song of birds, especially the nightingale, of which we shall have something to say in the next chapter. If indeed this is the case, the nightingale knows from natural instinct alone the various notes: the tractus, the subtractus, the contractus, and postractus; the high and the low; the plain, the joined, and the separate—and it teaches its art to the other small birds as they listen. Others say music was discovered from the buffeting of the wind in the vaulted forest, where there are certain sweet rustlings to be heard, especially at night. Others say from the sound of waters and the striking of wind upon cliffs and other rocky places: whence the line "his voice is as the voice of many waters." Others

3. Apparently the ultimate source (by way of Peter Comestor) is not Josephus, but Lucretius, *De rerum natura* 5.1252–61. This fact is of considerable interest since Lucretius was unknown for most of the Middle Ages until his rediscovery by Poggio in the early fifteenth century. I am indebted to Charles Segal of Harvard University for pointing out the Lucretian passage.
4. The passage appears in Isidore's *Etymologies* 3.16 (this volume, p. 40).

say it is clear from the Toledan tables that music originates from the violent motion of the peripheries of the heavens, that is, the revolution of the spheres either along their axes or in some manner along the shining rays of the sun.[5] Others, finally, say music originates from the stretched gut fibers of dead animals, separated from flesh and bone, particularly in flowing water or elsewhere.

Nonetheless one must agree with Hebraic truth that the original discoverer was Tubal, while various others, following him in both rank and lineage, up to the present time, produced new theories and findings, of which we shall speak below, and added these to the earlier discoveries, as is clear enough from other sciences. If indeed, as Priscian has it, while there are at first the elders, the youngers perceive with correspondingly greater penetration, as is clear from the ancient philosophers, then Socrates, then Plato, and finally Aristotle the Younger at the time of Alexander the Great.

CHAPTER II: ON THE BENEFITS THAT FOLLOW FROM THE INVENTION OF MUSIC

The ancients have made clear that the benefits of the musical art were so rich, that it would be, in the words of Isidore, as shameful to be ignorant of music as of letters. Hence music was never absent from sacrificial rites, from weddings, from banquets, or from war. And what was more remarkable, it was always present at burials. As blessed Isidore says, if the discipline of music be lacking, no discipline will be complete. Music stirs feeling, stimulates the senses, and animates warriors; indeed the more fierce the sound, the braver the soul in battle. Music gladdens the sorrowful, and it strikes fear in the guilty when the trumpet of the enemy sounds in their ears. Music lightens the labors of shepherds and of others, and braces those who languish; it calms agitated souls, banishes care and anxiety, and restrains and curbs violence. Moreover, to cite Isidore briefly, it miraculously draws beasts and snakes, birds and dolphins, to harken to its strains. And what is more marvellous, it casts out evil spirits from the body, banishing them by a certain miraculous and hidden divine power. If indeed, as we read, the Most High rightly allows demons to inhabit human bodies because of man's inclination to numerous vices, nevertheless when soothing melody moves the body to the opposite inclination, say, from severe depression to joy, the evil spirit departs. Whence the master of the *Historia scholastica* says that according to the magicians many demons cannot

---

5. This extremely difficult sentence compresses several elements of thirteenth-century Ptolemaic-Aristotelian astronomy. The Toledan tables, developed from Arabian astronomy, permitted one to calculate the position of the various heavenly bodies for every day of the year. The peripheries of the heavens (the supralunary spheres), in addition to their natural circular motion, have a "violent" motion, that is, one that is not natural but is caused by some agency such as a planetary intelligence. Musical sound is produced by the contrast between these two motions, the natural circular one and the "violent" one, which moves either inward along the axis of the universe to its earthly center or outward to the sun. I am indebted to Professor Catherine Tachau of Iowa University for her help with both the translation and the astronomical background.

endure harmony, and indeed none can when a fortuitous change in disposition is wrought through harmony in the bodies in which they dwell.[6] Whence the divinely inspired histories relate in the First Book of Kings, Chapter 15, that when the evil spirit vexed Saul, his servants said to him "take unto yourself a player *(psaltem)* who is skilled on the lyre" (by a *psaltes* one understands someone skilled in music), "and you will be relieved."[7] And it happened, then, that David played before Saul on the lyre whenever Saul was vexed by the demon, and Saul was relieved and refreshed, and the evil spirit departed from him (he is a spirit by nature, but evil through his own fault). The philosopher Asclepiades also restored a certain crazed man to his originally healthy state of mind through concordant melody, as blessed Isidore attests.

What else? We know from observation that birds swiftly descend to hear a melody, and learn it gladly, and teach it to their pupils generously. Whence Pliny relates in Book 10 and Ambrose in the *Hexaemeron*, that the nightingale (also called the *luscinia* or *acredula*) is a bird rather small in body, but extraordinary in voice and song.[8] When she warms her eggs in the spring time, she consoles herself during the sleepless labor of the long night with pleasant melody, so that she is able to bring life to the eggs on which she sits, no less by the sweet strains than by the warmth of her body. Usually the nightingale bears six eggs; thus, according to Pliny, she twitters away with her song for fifteen consecutive days and nights without letup, as the leafy twigs of the nest become compressed.

It is worthy of admiration that in so slight a body there thrives so tenacious a spirit. And it is admirable, too, that from one music of such perfection there flows such a variety of song, which is now drawn out, now varied in its inflection, now clear and concise. It issues forth and it returns; it becomes faint, sometimes murmuring to itself; it is full, low, high, focused, repeated, and prolonged. In so little a throat there is as much variation of song as in all the refined instruments that the art of man has invented. The song of each nightingale is like that of no other; it is her own unique song. Nightingales compete among themselves in a lively public contest. When conquered by death a nightingale often gives up its life with its breath departing before its song. The younger birds study the sweetness of the nightingale's song, taking in songs which they imitate. The student listens with rapt attention and repeats the corrections, now by singing, now by listening in silence, and now by beginning the song again. The nightingale wastes little time in eating so that she can enjoy the beauty of her own song. Thus she dies sometimes from singing, and in dying sings. Occasionally she is observed to exchange the sweetness of her song with that of a musical instrument, and in order to sing more vigorously she frequently closes her eyes. But this exquisite music gradually begins to leave off after fifteen days, and the color of the nightingale, just like her song, is

6. Peter Comestor, *Historia scholastica, Liber I Regum, XVI.*

7. 1 Kings (1 Samuel) 16:14–16.

8. Pliny, *Historia naturalis* 10.43; Ambrose, *Hexaemeron* 6.24.

altered little by little. There is not to be seen in the winter what existed in the spring, as both song and coloring have changed. But when reared in the refined surroundings of the palace, she renders her melodies not only in spring, but also in winter, and not just by day but also by night, as she is instructed equally by artifice and by nature.

Melody gives pleasure not only to what flies, that is birds, and to what walks, that is, animals, but to what swims, that is fish. Whence learned men tell marvellous things about the attraction of music for fish, and especially dolphins. Thus blessed Isidore says in Book 12 of the *Etymologies* that dolphins are called *simones,* because they follow the voices of men, or because they come together in flocks to hear the sound of a musical instrument. And then Pliny in Book 9 says the dolphin is the fastest of all animals, not only of the sea but of the land as well. It is faster than a bird, swifter than an arrow; it flies past ships driven by the wind; no type of fish is able to escape it, nor can anything else delay it, unless it be because it always takes its prey while bent over backwards, since its mouth is on its belly and its eyes on its back. Its voice is like the sighing of humans, its tongue like that of a pig, while its spine is cartilaginous. Like the whale it does not produce eggs; nor does it manufacture gall. A dolphin lives for 140 years; this was learned from severing the tail of a particular dolphin at the proper time. But some live longer, and others not so long, as is the case with other animals.

A dolphin is pregnant for ten months, and the young dolphin grows for ten years. It breathes and snorts, which is contrary to the nature of other fish. It has its penis within, rather than projecting without. It does not have breasts above its genitalia, but near its joints,[9] while the organ in which the fetus lies is quite hidden (the dolphin gives birth only during the summer). It walks on the bed of the sea, with its young following behind. It takes in water through its nostrils like swimming things, and air through its lungs like land animals. Its food it takes bending over backwards. Its testicles are enclosed within, not protruding without, like other fish of great size. According to the *Physiologus,* they cry wildly when caught; it is by song that they are enticed and captured. They kill crocodiles, too, by guile and deceit. They sleep on the water's surface. They are charmed by music. Now it happened once when some sailors were about to cast the citharist Arion into the sea, that he gained the concession from them that he first be permitted to play. A flock of dolphins were attracted by his song, and when he leap towards the water, he was caught by one of them and carried to the shore. Dolphins answer to those who call them *simones,* and they hearken to the words of man quicker than to the breath of the north wind, even though they have no ears, but rather some sort of apertures, which are somehow blocked when the south wind blows.

Dolphins revel in the music of tibias, and whenever they hear musical instruments playing they immediately turn to hear them, according to Solinus the

---

9. This obscure sentence appears to be defective in the manuscript.

philosopher in his *Book of Marvels*. He adds that there is a particular species of dolphin in the Nile who have saw-toothed crests on their backs: "They eagerly entice crocodiles to swim, and by a clever ruse swimming underneath them themselves, they slash their tender bellies and so slay them."[10] Enough has been said about the character of these animals in our book *On Natural History* and in our book on the characteristics of whatever particular fish.

10. Solinus, *De Mirabilibus* 13 and 23.

25 Marchetto of Padua

Marchetto makes his first appearance in history as *maestro di canto* at Padua Cathedral between 1305 and 1308. He completed his influential treatise on plainsong, *Lucidarium in arte musicae planae,* at Verona in 1318, and his equally influential treatise on mensural music, with the colorful title of *Pomerium in arte musicae mensuratae* (The Garden of Mensural Music), at Cesena in 1326. He was aided in the composition of both by the Dominican friar Syphans da Ferrara, which accounts for the abstract scholastic tone so evident in the excerpt from the *Pomerium* translated here. Nothing is known of Marchetto's life after 1326 except that he wrote a brief practical summary of his doctrine on mensural music, the *Brevis compilatio in arte musica.*

The *Pomerium* explains the notational system that was unique to Italy. Its most basic characteristic is that the breve remains a stable unit that is broken down into numerous "divisions" of semibreves and minims in order to accommodate the new rhythms of the fourteenth century. In the section of the treatise translated here, Marchetto deals with the divisions of imperfect time.

FROM *Pomerium in arte musicae mensuratae*

BOOK TWO: OF IMPERFECT TIME

Since the discipline of music has to do with opposites, let us also, now that we have considered perfect time in mensurable music, treat the subject of imperfect time in a similar manner. And in doing so, let us proceed in the following order. We shall treat: first, of imperfect time in itself and absolutely,

TEXT: Joseph Vecchi, ed., *Marchetti de Padua Pomerium*, Corpus Scriptorum de Musica, no. 6 (Rome: American Institute of Musicology, 1961), pp. 157–81. Translation by Oliver Strunk, revised by James McKinnon. The music examples of the last chapter are those taken by Strunk from the *Brevis compilatio.*

insofar as the comprehension of its essence is concerned; second, of imperfect time in its application to notes according to its totality and multiplication; third, of imperfect time in its application to notes according to its partibility and division.

I. OF IMPERFECT TIME IN ITSELF AND ABSOLUTELY

1. WHAT IMPERFECT TIME IS, SPEAKING MUSICALLY

In the first place we say that imperfect musical mensurable time is that which is a minimum, not in fullness, but in semi-fullness of voice. We demonstrate this definition as follows. It is certain that just as the perfect is that which lacks nothing, so the imperfect is that which lacks something. But it is also certain, by the definition of perfect time already demonstrated, that perfect time is that which is a minimum in entire fullness of voice, formed in the manner there expounded.[1] It follows, therefore, that imperfect time, since it falls short of perfect, is not formed in entire fullness of voice.

But someone may say: you ought to derive the deficiency of imperfect time with respect to perfect, not from fullness of voice, but from a lesser degree of time; and you ought, then, to say that both times, perfect as well as imperfect, are formed in fullness of voice, but that fullness of voice is formed in less time when it is formed in imperfect time than when it is formed in perfect. Whence, so they say, that minimum which is formed in fullness of voice is imperfect time, not perfect.

But to this we reply that to be in fullness of voice and to be a minimum is necessarily perfect time, for perfect musical time is the first measure of all, so that the measure of imperfect time is derived from it by subtracting a part, as will presently be explained. Therefore, since the minimum in any genus is the measure of all other things within it, as previously observed,[2] we conclude that minimum time is always perfect of itself, provided it be formed in fullness of voice; for as soon as we subtract from fullness of voice, we subtract from the quantity of perfect time and thus create imperfect time. So it appears that to define time by fullness of voice is to define it by essential plenitude or deficiency. Therefore our definition stands, namely that imperfect time is that which is a minimum, not in fullness of voice, but in semi-fullness. So much for the first point.

2. HOW PERFECT AND IMPERFECT TIME ARE ESSENTIALLY OPPOSED

Perfect and imperfect time are essentially opposed in themselves, absolutely, and without reference to any division or multiplication of either. This is sufficiently clear from our definition, but we shall, nevertheless, demonstrate it also. It is certain that perfect and imperfect time are not entirely the same thing, for if they were, imperfect time could be called essentially perfect, and

---

1. See Vecchi, p. 77, where Marchetto names Franco as his authority for this definition.
2. See ibid., where Marchetto refers this statement to the authority of Aristotle.

vice versa. Therefore they differ essentially. Now if two things differ essentially they differ actually, for the one is not the other. In this case they are opposed through "privation," for the one actually has something that the other has not. And from this it follows also that they are contradictory, for the same thing can never be true of both at the same time. There can, then, be no time which could at once be essentially and actually perfect and imperfect.

And if someone says: there could be a sort of time which for various reasons was at once perfect and imperfect; we reply that something or nothing would correspond to these reasons. If nothing would correspond, so much for the objection; if something, then one thing would be two things at the same time, which is impossible. It is therefore impossible for any musical time to be at once actually and essentially perfect and imperfect, as some pretend, for this implies a manifest contradiction: it amounts to saying that someone is both man and not man. So much for the second point.

3. BY HOW MUCH IMPERFECT TIME FALLS SHORT OF PERFECT

Imperfect time falls short of perfect by a third part, something we demonstrate as follows. It is certain that imperfect time is not as great in quantity as perfect, for if it were, it would not be imperfect. It is therefore necessary that it fall short of it by some quantity. It can, moreover, not fall short by less than one part, for if you say by half a part, that half a part will be one part, even though it would be half of the remainder. Therefore, since the primary and principal parts of perfect time are three, for it was divided above in a ternary division to obtain what is primary and principal, imperfect time, if it falls short of perfect, cannot do so by less than a third part. It follows, therefore, that imperfect time comprehends in itself and essentially two parts of perfect time.

II. OF THE APPLICATION OF IMPERFECT TIME TO NOTES ACCORDING TO ITS TOTALITY AND MULTIPLICATION

Imperfect time, of itself and according to its totality and multiplication, is altogether and completely similar to perfect in its application to notes. Notes of three tempora, of two tempora, and of one tempus occur in the same way in imperfect time as in perfect and are also similarly notated. All accidents of music in imperfect time, such as rests, tails, and dots, are treated just as in perfect time.

The reason is this: since there can never be intellectual knowledge, nor even sensible perception, of imperfect things, except by comparison to what is perfect (for never, whether through the intellect or through the senses, can we know a thing to be imperfect unless we also know what is needed to make it perfect); so science, as regards those things that are apprehended either by the intellect or the senses, has always to do with the perfect. Music, therefore, both with regard to its notes and with regard to its accidents, has always to do primarily and principally with perfect time. But by a subtraction made by the intellect of a part of perfect time, music becomes a science of imperfect time.

For if imperfect time were to have its own notes and accidents, different from those of perfect time, it follows that there would be a proper science of imperfect things, principally one of sense perception with no relation to what is perfect, something which, as we have said, is impossible both according to the intellect and according to the senses.

And if you say: very well, I shall be guided by the perfect, namely by comparing to its notes and accidents those of imperfect time; we reply that this will be in vain, for in such a comparison you could work only with the notes and accidents of perfect time, namely by subtracting fullness and in consequence quantity from them. Thus you would create notes and accidents of imperfect time in vain.

But one might ask: how am I to know when music is in perfect time and when in imperfect if, as you say, they are completely alike both in their notes and in their accidents? We reply that this is to be left entirely to the judgment of the composer, who understands the science of music thoroughly. In order, however, that one may know when the composer wishes the music to be sung in perfect time and when in imperfect, we say that when they are combined some sign ought to be added at the beginning of the music so that by means of it the wish of the composer who has arranged this varied music might be known. For as concerns the figured music and the notes no natural difference can be discovered.

It has been demonstrated that any written composition can be sung in either perfect or imperfect time. This difference in the manner of singing is provided by the composer alone, for the sake of the harmony. And because it depends entirely upon the will of the composer, and not upon the nature of the music, a sign that indicates the difference need be added only when the composer so wishes, nor can any valid reason be found why one sign is preferable to another. For some use p and i to indicate the perfect and imperfect; others 3 and 2 to indicate the ternary and binary divisions of the tempus; others use other signs according to their good pleasure.

But since every composition of itself and naturally observes perfect time more than imperfect (since one is called perfect, the other imperfect), music is by its nature inclined, not toward imperfect time, but toward perfect. It is because of the wish of the composer for a particular manner of composition that music observes imperfect time, abandoning perfect; and for this reason it must be the composer who adds the sign indicating that he intends the music to be in imperfect rather than perfect time.

III. OF THE APPLICATION OF IMPERFECT TIME TO NOTES ACCORDING TO ITS PARTIBILITY AND DIVISION

1. INTO HOW MANY PRINCIPAL PARTS IMPERFECT TIME IS DIVIDED

According to its partibility and division, imperfect time is so applied to notes that by primary division it is divided into two parts. Nor can it be divided into more, something we demonstrate as follows. It was shown in our first book that perfect time is divided (by primary division) into three parts, no more, no less; we say by primary and perfect division for reasons already adduced. At the beginning of this second book it was also shown that imperfect time falls short of perfect and, as was likewise shown there, that it cannot fall short by less than a third part. There remain, then, two parts of imperfect time. It is clear, therefore, that by primary division imperfect time can be divided only into two parts, for otherwise it would in no respect fall short of perfect. And this is logical and appropriate, for just as the perfect division corresponds to perfect time, which is into three, no more, no less, and this division comprehends all others; so the imperfect division corresponds to imperfect time, which is into two. And just as imperfect division is a part constituted within the ternary division, so imperfect time is a part constituted within perfect time.

In the first division of imperfect time, then, two semibreves and not more are the standard [*the divisio binaria*]. They have the same value and significance as two of the three semibreves of the first division of perfect time [*the divisio ternaria*]. For this reason they ought to be similarly notated, like this ◆ ◆, for they are equal to one another in value and in nature.

2. OF THE SECONDARY DIVISION OF IMPERFECT TIME, CONSIDERED IN ONE WAY

But if either of the two semibreves is given a descending tail, ◆ ◆ = ♩· ♪, ◆ ◆ = ♪♩·, we go on to the second division of imperfect time [*division quaternaria*], which is the division of each of our two parts into two others and not into three. For we have already explained and shown that imperfect time first observes imperfect division. And if afterwards we were to divide our primary parts first into three, it would be necessary to return to twos; and wishing to show how twos relate to threes, it would be necessary to repeat what we have said about threes. First let us say, then, that our parts of imperfect time are initially divided into two others, making four. These four are equal in nature, and they equal eight parts of the twelve-part division of perfect time [*divisio duodenaria perfecta*]: ◆ ◆ ◆ ◆ = ♩♩♩♩ .

But if only three of the four be given, the Italian practice is that the final one, being the end, will equal the first two. But if either one of the others be given a tail, the final one and the one without a tail will retain their natural value, the one with a tail equaling, by art, the two others: ◆ ◆ ◆ = ♩ ♫ , ◆ ◆ ◆ = ♪ ♩ ♪. With three notes, two cannot be given tails, for the second one with a tail would be meaningless. And with four notes, if we remain in this division, it is unnecessary to give tails to any; if it be done, the note with a tail will belong either to the secondary division of the primary parts, which is the division of each of two into three [*divisio senaria imperfecta*], or to the third division of imperfect time, which is the division of each of four into two [*divisio octonaria*]. In this case the proportion between the notes with ascending and descending tails and those without, and between the final notes and the preceding ones, both by art and by nature, is arrived at throughout as was amply demonstrated in our chapter on the semibreves of perfect time, and they will also be given the same names.

3. ON THE SECONDARY DIVISION OF IMPERFECT TIME CONSIDERED IN ANOTHER WAY

The principal parts of imperfect time, of which there are two, can each be divided into three, thus constituting six notes [*divisio senaria imperfecta*], and these six can again be divided in twos, making twelve [*divisio duodenaria imperfecta*], or in threes, making eighteen [*divisio octodenaria imperfecta*]. They are thus similar to the parts of the above described perfect time in the manner in which they are written and proportioned—in short, in all accidents, even in their names.

4. THE REFUTATION OF A CERTAIN ERROR

A serious error in mensurable music has arisen from what has just been stated. For some have maintained: you say that I can divide the two parts of imperfect time in threes and thus have six. But six also results from dividing the three parts of perfect time in twos. Therefore (our critics conclude) the *divisio senaria* is a mean between perfect and imperfect time.

We reply that, in dividing two things, a given number can always be found in both, and yet no part of either can ever be a mean between the one thing and the other; similarly, in dividing two lines by binary, ternary, and quaternary division, a given division can always be found in both, and yet no part of either can ever be a mean between the one line and the other. Thus, whenever you divide imperfect time into its parts, you hit upon the same number of parts as you will in dividing perfect time into its parts. Nevertheless, no part of imperfect time can ever be a mean between itself and perfect time, nor can all its parts together, because the nature of imperfect time differs from that of perfect time in itself and essentially, something that is altogether obvious in their performance.[3]

And if someone says: you claim that only the imperfect falls short of the perfect; we reply that this is true by the proportion of perfect time to imperfect, for in their essences the two times are distinct from one another, separate and opposite, as is clear from their opposed definitions, one being formed only in fullness of voice, the other in semi-fullness.

---

3. See ibid., 84, where Marchetto makes the same point, invoking the authority of Aristotle, *Metaphysics* 1057A.

5. ON THE GREAT DIFFERENCE BETWEEN THE SINGING OF THE FRENCH AND ITALIANS IN IMPERFECT TIME, AND ON WHO SINGS MORE RATIONALLY

Be it known that there is a great difference between the Italians and the French in the manner of proportioning notes when singing in imperfect time. The Italians always attribute perfection to the end, as results from proportioning the notes in the manner of singing in perfect time; while the French attribute perfection to the beginning. Thus the Italians say that the final note is more perfect, since it is the end, but the French say the opposite: they say that while this is true of perfect time, in imperfect time the final note is always less perfect, since it is the end.

Which nation, then, sings more rationally? The French, we reply. The reason is that just as in anything perfect its last complement is said to be its perfection with respect to its end (for the perfect is that which lacks nothing, not only with respect to its beginning, but also with respect to its end), so in anything imperfect its imperfection and deficiency is understood with respect to its end (for a thing is called imperfect when it lacks something with respect to its end). If, therefore, we wish to sing or proportion notes in the manner of singing in imperfect time, we ought rationally to attribute imperfection always to the final note, just as in the manner of singing in perfect time we attribute perfection to it. From this we conclude that in the manner of singing the French sing better and more reasonably than the Italians.

The manner of the Italians can, however, be supported by saying that they imitate perfection in so far as they can (which is reasonable enough), namely by always reducing the imperfect to the perfect. Then, since the proportion of imperfect time is reduced to the perfection of perfect time (which amounts to reducing the imperfect to the perfect), the singing of the Italians in imperfect time can be supported reasonably enough. Thus it must be maintained, for the reason already given, that the French sing better and more properly, but, again on the grounds already established, it is reasonable enough to accept the singing of the Italians.

6. OF THE NAMES AND PROPERTIES OF THE SEMIBREVES OF IMPERFECT TIME IN THE FRENCH AND THE ITALIAN MANNER.[4]

If two semibreves are taken for the imperfect tempus, in both the French and the Italian manners they are performed alike:

---

4. Marchetto's description in this section of the French manner of dividing the imperfect tempus agrees with that of Philippe de Vitry; see Gilbert Reaney, et al., eds., *Philippi de Vitriaco Ars Nova*, Corpus Scriptorum de Musica, no. 8 (Rome: American Institute of Musicology, 1964), p. 23.

And since they are parts of the first division of imperfect time [*divisio binaria*] they are called, by nature, major semibreves, because they are comparable to two semibreves of the first division of perfect time [*divisio ternaria*]. By art, however, one of them can be given a tail; and then, in the Italian manner, we go on to the second division of imperfect time [*divisio quaternaria*], which is the division into four equal semibreves. Since this second division of imperfect time is comparable in a partial way to the second division of perfect time [*divisio senaria perfecta*], which is the division into six, its four equal semibreves are called minor semibreves by nature. And the semibreve with a tail, which is called major by art, will contain three of four parts, while the one without a tail retains its natural value:

But in the French manner, if one is given a tail, we go on at once to the ternary division of imperfect time [*divisio senaria imperfecta*], which is the division into six equal semibreves. These are called minims in the first degree, because the semibreves have been divided beyond the division of minor semibreves. In this case the semibreve with a tail contains five of six parts by art, while the one without a tail retains its natural value.

If three semibreves are taken for the imperfect tempus, in the Italian manner the final one, since it is the end, will equal the two others in value:

But in the French manner, in order that the proportion and perfection of the whole measure may be preserved, the first note will contain three of six parts, the second will contain two, and the third one, the notes being called major semibreve, minor semibreve, and minim.

When there are four semibreves, in the Italian manner they are performed alike:

But in the French manner (for in dividing imperfect time the French do not go beyond the *divisio senaria,* even though they could) the first of these four contains two parts of six and the second contains one; while the other two make up the second half of the perfection, with the third containing two parts and the fourth one, which fills out the second half of the perfection. This way of proportioning four notes among the six parts of the tempus was altogether necessary in order that the French form might be observed. For, as will appear upon reflection, in no other way can such a proportion or perfection be worked out without an excess or deficiency of perfection. If each of the first two notes contained two parts of the tempus, and each of the remaining two contained only one, there would be no proportion between the parts, since in a division of this kind no mean proportion can ever rationally and naturally be found. This we refer to as by nature, for by art the same result can be obtained by adding the sign of art.

When there are five semibreves, in the Italian manner they belong to the fourth division of imperfect time [*divisio octonaria*], which is the division into eight, comparable in a partial way to the division of perfect time into twelve [*divisio duodenaria perfecta*]. The first two will be called minims in the second degree, while the others remain in the second division of imperfect time:

By art, however, these minims can be placed otherwise among the five:

But in the French manner the first three are equal minims by nature, while the fourth contains two parts, and the fifth one. For always when there are more than four semibreves, they take the first three minims for half of a tempus, and after this they place the more perfect immediately before the less perfect, proportioning them one to the other. Thus it ought always to be understood that the French attribute perfection to the beginning.

When there are six semibreves, in the Italian manner the first four are minims, measured as four of the eight parts of the tempus, while the last two remain in the second division:

But it is our wish that, however these minims are placed in the Italian manner, whether at the beginning or at the end, they always have tails added above:

The reason for this is that the Italians, as we said above, pass to the fourth division of the tempus, which is in eight, after the second division, which is in four, and never remain naturally in six.

But in the French manner all are equal and, as we have said before, they are called minims.

When there are seven semibreves, in the Italian manner the first six contain six parts of the tempus, while the last one remains in the second division:

unless it happens that the six are artificially distinguished:

When there are eight semibreves, all are performed alike as minims:

But in the French manner, if one wished to take more than six semibreves for the imperfect tempus, he would fall at once into its third division [*divisio duodenaria imperfecta*], which is the division of six into twelve, so that some of them would require ascending tails.

But someone might ask: how can I know which of the semibreves with ascending tails belong to the third division (in twelve), and which to the second division (in six), when with six also various notes are given ascending tails? We reply that this depends on whether the number of notes is less or greater than six.

And in order that it may be known which division of imperfect time we ought to follow in singing mensurable music, whether the French or the Italian, we say that at the beginning of any composition in the French manner, above the sign of imperfect time which appears there, one should place a G, denoting or indicating that the composition should be performed in the French manner (just as in plainsong the founders of music placed a gamma at the beginning of the Guidonian hand to show that we had music from the Greeks), for we had this division of the imperfect tempus from the French. And if a single composition in imperfect time be proportioned according to the French and Italian manners combined, we say that at the beginning of the part in the French manner there should be placed a G, but that in a similar way at the beginning of the part in the Italian manner there should be placed a Greek I [our Y], which is the initial of their name.

26 Jehan des Murs

Born in Normandy about 1300, Jehan is cited in 1318 as a baccalaureate student in the Faculty of Arts at Paris. He spent the next several years in Paris, until about 1325, completing his master's degree and writing the bulk of his works on music. He moved frequently during his well-documented but not particularly distinguished career, occupying ecclesiastical and academic positions occasionally in Paris but more often in cities of his native Normandy, and even in Avignon. The last firm date in his biography is 1345, suggesting that he died about mid-century.

Jehan wrote astronomical and mathematical works, but his treatises on music were considerably more influential. There are at least three genuine works and perhaps as many as six, copied in some 125 manuscripts of the fourteenth and fifteenth centuries. Jehan's exposition of the rhythmical innovations of the early fourteenth century, the so-called *ars nova,* was as authoritative for its subject as was that of Franco of Cologne for his. Translated here is the section of the *Notitia artis musicae (Ars novae musicae),* completed in 1321, which summarizes these innovations.

FROM *Notitia artis musicae*

BOOK TWO: MUSICA PRACTICA

Since we touched lightly and briefly on the theory of music in the preceding discourse, it now remains to inquire at greater length into its practice, that part which is mensurable, since different practitioners think differently about this. As was shown in Book 1, sound is generated by motion, because it belongs to the class of successive things.[1] For this reason it exists while it is being made, but it no longer exists once it has been made. Succession does not exist without motion. Time inseparably unites motion. Therefore it follows necessarily that time is the measure of sound. Time is also the measure of motion. But for us time is the measure of sound prolonged in one continuous motion, and we apply this same definition of time to the single *tempus.*

According to one account, there are two sorts of time—greater and lesser, greater time having longer motion, lesser time shorter. These do not, however, differ in species, for greater and lesser quantities do not alter species. Our predecessors reasonably attributed a certain mode of perfection to every tempus of measured sound; they prescribed the sort of tempus that would be subject to a ternary division, for they believed all perfection to be in the ternary number. Thus they established perfect time as the measure of all music, for they knew that it is unsuitable for the imperfect to be found in art. Yet certain moderns believe themselves to have discovered the opposite of this, which is not consistent. Their meaning will be more clearly set forth in what follows.

2. ON THE PERFECTION OF THE TERNARY NUMBER

That all perfection lies in the ternary number follows from many likely reflections. In God, who is most perfect, there is one substance, yet three per-

---

TEXT: Ulrich Michels, ed., *Johannis de Muris Notitia Artis Musicae,* Corpus Scriptorum de Musica, no. 17 (Rome: American Institute of Musicology, 1972), pp. 65–87; 106–107. Translation by Oliver Strunk, revised by James McKinnon.

1. See Michels, p. 50.

sons; he is threefold, yet one, and one, yet threefold. Very great, therefore, is the correspondence of unity to trinity. In knowledge, one finds (after God) in a ternary series: being, essence, and their composite. In the first of corporeal entities, the heavens, there are the thing that moves, the thing that is moved, and time. There are three attributes in the stars and the sun—heat, light, and splendor; in the elements—action, passion, and matter; in individuals—generation, corruption, and dissolution; in all finite time—beginning, middle, and end; and in all curable disease—rise, climax, and decline. There are three intellectual operations; three terms in the syllogism; three figures in argument; three intrinsic principles of natural things; three potentialities of the being that has not suffered privation; three loci of correlative distance; and three lines in the whole universe. The ternary number is the first uneven number (the first number is first and incomposite). Not two lines, but three, enclose a surface; the first of all polygonal figures is the triangle; and the first of all rectilinears is the triangular. Every object, if it is ever to stand, has three dimensions.

Now, since the ternary number is everywhere present in some form or other, it may no longer be doubted that it is perfect. And, by the contrary of this proposition, the binary number, since it falls short of the ternary and is of lesser repute, remains imperfect. But any composite number formed from these may properly be considered perfect because of its similarity and correspondence to the ternary. And time, since it belongs to the class of continuous things, is divisible not only by ternary numbers, but is endlessly divisible—to infinity.

Seeing, on the other hand, that sound measured by time consists in the union of two forms, namely the natural and the mathematical, it follows that because of the one its division never ceases, while because of the other its division must necessarily stop somewhere; for just as nature limits the magnitude and increase of all material things, so it also limits their minuteness and decrease. For natural things demonstrate that nature is limited by a maximum and a minimum. Sound, moreover, is in itself a natural form to which quantity is artificially attributed; it is necessary, therefore, for there to be limits of division beyond which no sound, however fractionable, may go. These limits we wish to apprehend by reason.

3. ON THE LIMITS OF DIVIDING SOUND

Prolonged sound measured by definite time is formed in the air not so much in the likeness of a point, line, or surface, as rather bodily and spherically (in the likeness of a sphere, as light is formed in free space), something which may be tested by six listeners placed according to the six differences of proportion. And since such a sound is set in motion by the force of the strike that produces it, which is finite since it proceeds from a finite body, its duration and continuation are necessarily limited, for a sound cannot be generated in infinity or in an instant. Its limits are disposed in the following way.

All music, especially mensurable music, is founded in perfection, combining in itself number and sound. The number, moreover, which musicians consider perfect in music is, as follows from what has been said, the ternary number. Music, then, takes its origin from the ternary number. The ternary number multiplied by itself produces nine; in a certain sense this ninefold number contains every other, for beyond nine there is always a return to the unit. Music, then, does not go beyond the nine-part number. Now the nine-part number again multiplied by itself produces 81, a product which is measured by the ternary number in three dimensions, just as sound is. For if we take three by three by three by three, or three threes nine times, with the products of three always multiplied by three; then, as 3 times 3 produces 9, and 3 times 9 produces 27, so 3 times 27 produces 81. From the unit, then, the third part of the ternary number, which is perfect, to 81, which is likewise perfect—these are said to be the maximum and minimum limits of any sound, for the entire duration of a sound is included between these extremes.

Within these limits, four distinct degrees of perfection may rationally be apportioned. They are the following. No musical perfection exceeds the ternary number; it embraces perfection within itself. A perfection is that according to which something is called perfect. Perfect is that which is divisible into three equal parts, or into two unequal ones, of which the larger is twice the smaller. Unity, moreover, is indivisible and may be called neutral. In these, then, is comprehended the genus of divisibility and likewise of indivisibility. Now, 81 is ternary and in this respect perfect; 54 is the corresponding binary number and in this respect imperfect; the corresponding unit is 27 which makes the perfect imperfect and the imperfect perfect. In these three numbers we distinguish the first degree of perfection; from 27 to 9 we distinguish the second; from 9 to 3 the third; and from 3 to 1 the fourth. In any one of these we find the ternary, the binary, and the unitary, that is, the perfect, the imperfect, and the neutral. There are then four degrees, no more, no less.

4. On the Extension of the Notational Figures

We have still to show by what figures, signs, or notes the things which we have said may be appropriately indicated or represented, and by what words or names they may be called, for at this very time our doctors of music dispute daily with one another about this. And although signs are arbitrary, yet, since all things should somehow be in mutual agreement, musicians ought to devise signs more appropriate to the sounds signified. In devising these, all the wiser ancients long ago agreed that geometrical figures should be the signs of musical sounds; and they wished to call them points, not, however, as if indivisible, but like a day, just as the physician does today.[2] The figure most suitable for writing

2. The difficult second clause of this sentence, along with two other passages that follow closely, were omitted by Strunk (see Michels, p. 109 on the subject of their authenticity). Its precise meaning eludes the present editor, who suggests only that Jehan, in contrasting something indivisible with a day, may have had in mind the principle that he stated in Chapter 2 above—that time is endlessly divisible.

music is the plane quadrilateral, for it is created by a single stroke of the pen. In it, every musical note shape coverges, as if within a genus, and through it, varied in its essential forms, every mode of any song is explained. When I say "by essential," I refer to the "natural" forms of the figure, after it has been named, or to the "essential" forms, that is, those of the essential shape of the note, the figure that expresses meaning.[3] The musical note is a quadrilateral figure arbitrarily representative of numbered sound measured by time. There are nine distinctions of this form: rectangularity, equilaterality, the tail, the dot, the position, the right side, the left side, the upward direction, and the downward direction as will be seen in the diagram to follow.

Now the ancients, while they wrote reasonably about the figures of the second and third degrees, had little to say about the first and fourth, although they made use of these remote degrees in their singing. For reasons which we shall pass over, their figures did not adequately represent what they sang. Nevertheless they gave us the means of accomplishing completely what they had incompletely accomplished. For they decided that the ternary and binary would be represented by the same figure, and the unit by a dissimilar one, inasmuch as the binary is closer to the ternary than the unit is. For the intellect takes those things that are close to be the same, and it passes more readily between things that have a common symbol[4] (and conversely). From the ternary to the binary, that is, from perfect to imperfect, and vice versa, one passes more readily than from the ternary to the unit; whatever the degree, therefore, the more similar figure ought to be common to those things the distinction between which is not perceived in themselves but is manifest rather in their relation to another thing.

In the second degree, according to our predecessors, the quadrilateral, equilateral, rectangular figure with a tail to the right, ascending or descending, represented perfect and imperfect alike, that is, the ternary and binary. The same figure without a tail represented the unit in the second degree, and the ternary and binary in the third degree; while the unit of the third degree was represented by the quadrilateral, equilateral, obtuse-angular figure.

As to the first degree, the earlier authorities spoke about the binary and the unit, omitting the ternary or representing it by a figure similar to the one denoting the binary. In the fourth they abandoned the unit entirely or figured

---

3. The second of the passages omitted by Strunk (beginning with "and through it"). The point of it appears to be a matter of fourteenth-century semiology derived from Roger Bacon. The different variations of the quadrilateral figure (the square shape of the breve, the lozenge shape of the semibreve, etc.) are not completely arbitrary; rather, they are signs chosen for some degree of innate (essential or natural) suitability. I am indebted to Catherine Tachau of Iowa University for this explanation.

4. The first clause of this sentence is the third of the passages omitted by Strunk; it offers no difficulties. As for the second clause, Strunk pointed out that it appears verbatim in Jacques of Liège (Roger Bragard, ed., *Jacobi Leodiensis Speculum Musicae,* Corpus Scriptorum de Musica, no. 3, Liber septimus [Rome, American Institute of Musicology, 1973], p. 72) in a different connection, suggesting that it might be a familiar axiom.

it implicitly in the ligatures. This is the last figure in the fourth degree, namely a quadrilateral, equilateral, obtuse-angular figure with a tail ascending. But in the first degree the first figure is similar to the second, namely a quadrilateral, non-equilateral, rectangular figure with a tail to the right, ascending or descending.

The differences of the first degree are between the non-equilateral figure and the equilateral; those of the second degree between the figure with a tail and the one without; those of the third between the rectangular figure and the obtuse-angular; those of the fourth between the obtuse-angular figure with a tail and the one without.

5. ON NAMING THE FIGURES

We have still to speak about the names of the figures that we call notes. In the first degree we can name them triplex long, duplex long, and simplex long. In the second, following the terminology of the ancients, perfect long, imperfect long, and breve. In the third, after the fashion of the preceding degree, perfect breve, imperfect breve, and semibreve (so named not from equal division, but from being greater or lesser, so that the binary is called the greater part of three, the unit the lesser part, the lesser semibreve having been so called by the ancients also). In the fourth degree, following the terminology of the preceding ones, perfect semibreve, imperfect semibreve, and least semibreve.

Others name the notes differently while retaining the same sense. Omitting those of the first degree, which are named appropriately enough, there might be long, semilong, and breve; breve, semibreve, and minor; minor, semiminor, and minim. Or more appropriately (and beginning with the unit of the first degree): longa, longior, longissima (or magna, major, maxima); then, in the second degree, longa perfecta, longa imperfecta, and brevis; then, brevis, brevior, and brevissima (or parva); and then, parva, minor, and minima.

All this is clear from the following table [opposite]:

6. ON THE PERCEPTION OF PERFECTION[5]

Perfection and imperfection are represented, as we have said, by the same figure, just as the same general material may appear in various forms; the authorities applied the distinction between them to five modes, as is evident in the second degree, the one about which they had the most to say. A long before a long is perfect, assigned the value of three *tempora;* so also is a long before two breves, before three breves, before a dot, and before a long rest. This distinction is called "from place or position." The imperfect long is recognized in two of these modes, by the preceding unit or by the following unit. What has been said of the second degree is to be understood of the other degrees in their own way.

5. Strunk's omission of three tables in this chapter is maintained in the present edition.

◗	3	81	longissima		first degree [maximodus]
◖	2	54	longior		
◗	1	27	longa	same	
◗	3	27	perfecta		second degree [modus]
◗	2	18	imperfecta		
■	1	9	brevis	same	
■	3	9	brevis		third degree [tempus]
■	2	6	brevior		
◆	1	3	brevissima	same	
◆	3	3	parva		fourth degree [prolatio]
◆	2	2	minor		
✦	1	1	minima		

Five *species* of melody can be distinguished in any one of these degrees: one entirely in perfect notes or with the binary preceding and the unit following (with corresponding rests), as though in the first mode;[6] a second species with the unit preceding and the binary following; a third combining the first and second, that is, with the perfect note preceding and two units following (the second of which represents a binary value with a unitary form); a fourth made in the opposite way; and a fifth composed entirely of units and their divisions.

Of rests and ligatures new things might be said, but let what is found in the canons of the ancients be sufficient to them, except that rests may now be arranged in the four degrees.

7. ON PERFECT AND IMPERFECT TIME

At the end of this little work be it observed that music may combine perfect notes in imperfect time (for example, notes equal in value to three breviores) with imperfect notes in perfect time (for example, notes equal in value to two

6. These *species* are clearly the five rhythmic modes as defined above by Franco of Cologne, *Ars cantus mensurabilis*, section 3 (this volume, pp. 118–19).

breves), for three binary values and two ternary ones are made equal in multiples of six. Thus three perfect binary values in imperfect time are as two imperfect ternary ones in perfect, and alternating one with another they are finally made equal by equal proportion.[7] And music is sung with perfect notes in perfect time, or with imperfect ones in imperfect, whichever is fitting.

Again, it is possible to separate and disjoin perfections, not continuing them, as when a single breve occurs between two perfect notes, yet, when the breves have been gathered together, the whole produces a perfection.[8] For whatever can be sung can be written down, so long as the notes are whole and proper.

There are, moreover, many other new things latent in music which will appear altogether plausible to posterity.

Certain things are included in this *Ars musicae* of ours that are somewhat obscured by being left implicit; if they were to be made explicit, they might silence many of those who dispute with one another on various points. I should like, then, more from love of the disputants than for the sake of accuracy, to assert in a consistent and appropriate way certain conclusions regarding which there has been considerable controversy. And let no invidious critic rise up against us if we are obliged to state what was unspoken, while preserving the modes and other obvious points, and maintaining always the bounds set by the ancients.

8. Conclusions

1. The long may be made imperfect by the breve.
2. The breve may be made imperfect by the semibreve.
3. The semibreve may be made imperfect by the minim.
4. The long may be made imperfect by the semibreve.
5. The breve may be made imperfect by the minim.
6. The minim may not be made imperfect.
7. The altered breve may be made imperfect by the semibreve.
8. The altered semibreve may be made imperfect by the minim.
9. The tempus may be divided into any number of equal parts.

•   •   •   •   •

15. Finis

In these nine stated conclusions there are implicit many other special ones that will be made clear to the student by their application.

If these few things which we have said include anything that seems to be inconsistent with the truth, we ask you, venerable musicians (you in whom we have delighted from earliest youth because of music, for no science is hidden from him who knows music well), how far, from love of this work, you will

---

7. Probably the first theoretical mention of the so-called *aequipollentiae;* the musical compositions of the fourteenth century generally represented this with red (or "colored") notes.
8. Probably the first theoretical mention of syncopation.

correct and charitably tolerate our defects. For it is not possible for the mind of one man, unless he have an angelic intellect, to comprehend the whole truth of any science. Perhaps in the course of time there will happen to us what is now happening to the ancients, who believed that they had spoken definitively about music. Let no one say that we have concealed the state of music or its immutable end. For knowledge and opinion move in cycles, revolving back upon themselves, as long as it pleases the supreme will of him who has freely created this world and of his own accord made discrete everything that is in it.

27 Jacques of Liège

Little is known of Jacques' life; he appears to have been born in Liège, perhaps about 1260, and to have studied at the University of Paris. He died in his native Liège, sometime after the completion of his *Speculum musicae* in about 1330. The *Speculum,* a profoundly conservative work, is the longest surviving medieval treatise on music, comprising seven books in 521 chapters. The first five books are devoted to *musica speculativa,* the sort of material dealt with in the Greek science of harmonics; here Boethius is Jacques' principal authority. The sixth book treats the ecclesiastical modes with Guido of Arezzo as principal authority, and the seventh treats discant and mensural music with Franco of Cologne serving in a similar capacity. It is in this final book, excerpted below, that Jacques engages in his famous attack on the innovations described by Jehan des Murs. Ironically, the *Speculum* was for many years attributed to Jehan.

FROM *Speculum musicae*

PROHEMIUM TO THE SEVENTH BOOK

In his commentary on the *Categories* of Aristotle, Simplicius says, by way of commending the ancients: "We are not at all adequate in our discernment of the true and the false, yet in this we delight—to attack our betters."[1]

Indeed, just as it is profitable and praiseworthy to imitate things well done by the ancients, so it is pleasant and commendable to approve things well said

TEXT: Roger Bragard, ed., *Jacobi Leodiensis Speculum Musicae*, Corpus Scriptum de Musica, no. 3, Liber septimus (Rome, American Institute of Musicology, 1973), pp. 5–7; 86–95. Translation by Oliver Strunk, revised by James McKinnon.

1. *Commentaria in Aristotelem graeca*, 8.8

by them; rather than to attack them, which seems to be the custom of the young especially, for though the young are more inventive, the old are conceded to be more judicious. As the Master says in his *Histories,* young and inexperienced persons, pleased by new things (for novelty is congenial and enchanting to the ear), ought not so to prize the new that they bury the old. For as a rule new teachings, although they glitter outwardly upon first acquaintance, are revealed to lack solid inner foundations when carefully examined; they are dismissed and soon drop out of favor. If, moreover, it be unprofitable to accomplish by many means what can conveniently be accomplished by few, what profit can there be in adding to a sound old doctrine a wanton and curious new one, repudiating the former? As it is written, "You shall not remove your neighbor's landmark, which the men of old have set."[2]

Long ago venerable men, among them Tubalcain from before the Flood, and since his time many more whom we have already mentioned, have discoursed on plainsong; while many others, among whom Franco the German and another referred to as Aristotle[3] stand out, have written on mensurable music. Now in our day new and more recent authors have appeared, who write on mensurable music with little reverence for their ancestors, the ancient doctors; to the contrary, they change their sound doctrine in many respects, corrupting, criticizing, annulling, and protesting against it in word and deed, whereas the civil and ethical thing to do would be to imitate the ancients in what they have said well and, in doubtful matters, to explain and defend them.

I was grieved when I reflected upon these things in the modern manner of singing and still more in the modern writings, and decided, therefore, to write something about mensurable music with the defense of the ancients as my primary and principal purpose, although, afterwards, as a secondary purpose and from necessity, I turned to plainsong and to theoretical and practical music. Having with God's help completed what was incidental, let me now, if I can, carry out my original design.

I ask the benevolent reader to have pity on me, and I beg him to hear me with sympathy, for to my regret I am alone, while those whom I attack in this last satiric and controversial work are many. I do not doubt that the modern way of singing and what is written about it displease many worthy persons, but yet I have not observed anyone to have written against them. I still belong to the ancient company which some of the moderns call rude. I am old; they are young and vigorous. Those whom I defend are dead; those whom I attack still living. They rejoice in having found nine new conclusions about mensurable music;[4]

---

2. Deuteronomy 19:14.

3. Lambertus, who composed a treatise on mensural music, *Tractatus de musica,* in Paris about 1270.

4. An obvious reference to the nine new conclusions of Jehan des Murs; there are a number of further references to Jehan in what follows.

I am content to defend the traditional ones, which I deem reasonable. "Knowledge and opinion move in cycles," they say, borrowing from Aristotle's *Meteorology;*[5] for now it is dry where before there was water.

We are not to ascribe to presumption what is done from love of truth and from loyalty, when the moderns themselves claim that they write from love of truth. Where there are two friends it is most sacred to honor truth. "Socrates is my friend, but truth is still more my friend."[6] Whence St. Jerome, in his epistle against Rufinus, says on the authority of Pythagoras: "After God, let us cultivate truth, which alone brings men close to God."[7] For he who deserts truth deserts God, since God is truth.

It still seems pious to honor the ancients, who have given us a foundation in mensurable music; and pious to defend them in what they have said well and, in doubtful matters, to explain them, not to attack them; as it seems uncivil and reprehensible to attack good men after they are dead and unable to defend themselves. Let what I have said be my apology. For though in this work I am about to speak against the teachings of the moderns (insofar as they oppose the teachings of the ancients), I delight in their persons, and I have from my youth delighted in song and singers, music and musicians.

•　　•　　•　　•　　•

45. A Comparison of the Old Art of Mensurable Music with the New, As Regards Perfection and Imperfection

As I near the end of this work, let me draw certain comparisons from what has already been said. Let none take offense; I have spoken and will continue to speak about things as I see them, without prejudice of any kind. The facts are in no way altered by any assertion or denial of mine. May what is reasonable or more reasonable and what accords more fully with this art be retained, and what is less reasonable be rejected. Since man lives by art and by reason, there must be a place in every man for what accords with art and reason. Reason follows the law of nature which God has implanted in rational creatures. But since imperfections have at last come to be discussed, let us now compare the ancient and modern arts of mensurable music with respect to perfection and imperfection.

To some, perhaps, the modern art will seem more perfect than the ancient, because it seems more subtle and more difficult. It appears to be more subtle because it reaches out further and makes many additions to the old art, as is evident in the notes and measures and modes (for the word subtle is used of that which is more penetrating, reaching out further). That it is more difficult

---

5. *Meteorology* 339B.

6. Proverbial, but ultimately derived from Aristotle, *Nicomachean Ethics* 1096A.

7. *Epistula adversus Rufinum* 39; pierre Lardet, ed., Corpus Christianorum Series Latina 79 (Turnholt: Brepols, 1982), p. 109.

may be seen in the manner of singing and of dividing the measure in the works of the moderns.

To others, however, the opposite seems true, for that art appears to be more perfect which follows its basic principle more closely and goes against it less. Now the art of mensural music is based on perfection, as not only the ancients but the moderns declare. Therefore whichever makes the greater use of perfection appears to be the more perfect; and this is true of the ancient art, the art of Master Franco.

For the new art, as we have seen, uses manifold and various imperfections in its notes, modes, and measures. Imperfection intrudes virtually everywhere: not content with imperfecting notes, modes, and measures, it extends itself to the tempus. For the new art has what it calls imperfect time, and has breves which it calls imperfect in regard to time, a thing unknown to the old art. And it applies an imperfection arising from time to the notes of the individual degrees: to simple, duplex, and also triplex longs; to breves, while some apply it even to semibreves.

The practitioners of this art are still inventing new ways of imperfecting what is perfect: by proximate or direct imperfection, when the perfect simple long is made imperfect by the breve; by remote, when the same note is made imperfect by the semibreve because it is the third part of a breve recta; and by more remote, when the same long is made imperfect by the minim. Nor are the moderns satisfied with making perfect notes imperfect and dragging them to imperfection; they must do this even with the imperfect notes, since they are not content with a single imperfection, but require many.

If the new art spoke of these imperfections only in a speculative way, it would be more tolerable; but not so, for they make excessive use of imperfection in practice. They employ more imperfect notes than perfect; more imperfect modes than perfect; and consequently more imperfect measures.

When it is said that the new art is more subtle than the ancient, it must be said also that, granting this, it is not therefore more perfect. For not all subtlety is proof of perfection, nor is greater subtlety proof of greater perfection. Subtlety has no place among the degrees or orders or species of perfection, as is made clear in the fifth book of the *Metaphysics*.[8] Nor is it sufficiently proven that the new art is more subtle than the old, even if we grant that it includes some new devices to which the old does not extend. That the new art includes many imperfections unknown to the old art does not prove it more perfect, but merely raises the question of which of the arts under discussion is the more perfect.

As to the further assertion that the modern art is more difficult than the ancient, this, it must be said, does not make it more perfect, for what is more difficult is not for that simple reason more perfect. Art, even if it is said to be concerned with what is difficult, is nevertheless concerned with what is good

8. Aristotle, *Metaphysics* 1021B.

and useful, since it is a virtue perfecting the soul through the medium of the intellect. For this reason authority says that the teaching of the wise is easy. But this will be discussed later on.

46. A COMPARISON OF THE OLD ART OF MENSURABLE MUSIC WITH THE NEW, AS REGARDS SUBTLETY AND RUDENESS

Some moderns regard those singers as rude, simpleminded, undiscerning, foolish, and ignorant who do not know the new art and who in singing follow the old art rather than the new; and in consequence they regard the old art as rude and, as it were, irrational, and the new as subtle and rational. But one might ask, what is the source of this subtlety in the moderns and this rudeness in the ancients? For if subtlety comes from a greater and more penetrating intellect, who are to be considered the more subtle: those who discovered the principles of this art and found out what things are contrary to them, but have scrupulously followed these principles, or those who protest their intention of following them but do not, and seem rather to combat them? Let the judicious observe without passion which party is offering a true judgment of this matter. And what is the value of subtlety, what the value of difficulty, without utility? What is the value of subtlety which is contrary to the principles of science? Are not the subtlety and difficulty involved in the many diverse imperfections in notes, times, modes, and measures which they have contrived, incompatible with a science which is based on perfection? Is it great subtlety to abound in imperfections and to dismiss perfections?

Should the ancients be called rude for using perfections, the moderns subtle for using imperfections? Should the moderns be called subtle for introducing triplex longs, for joining duplex longs in ligature, for using duplex longs profusely, for using semibreves singly, for providing them with tails, for giving them the power of making longs and breves imperfect and still another power which seems unnecessary to this art, and for many other innovations which seem to contradict its very foundation?

Should they be called subtle, moreover, for their new manner of singing, in which the words are lost, the effect of good concord is lessened, and the measure, as will be discussed later on, is confused? And who are those who use so many different sorts of music and manners of singing, who apply themselves to many distinct kinds of music and manners of singing? Do not the moderns use motets and chansons almost exclusively, except for introducing hockets into their motets? They have abandoned many other genres of music, not using them in their proper form as the ancients did; for example, measured organum, organum that is not measured throughout, and organum purum and duplum, which few of the moderns know; likewise the conductus, a song that is so beautiful and gives such pleasure, and which is similarly artful and delightful when duplex, triplex, or quadruplex; as is the case with duplex, contraduplex, triplex, and quadruplex hockets.

Among these types of song the singers of old divided their time in turn; these they made their foundation; in these they exercised themselves; and in these they delighted—not just in motets and chansons. Should they who understood and performed these kinds of music, or those who understand and perform them now, be called rude, foolish, and ignorant of the art of singing, because they do not sing the modern sorts of music or in the modern manner, and do not use the new art of the moderns? They would know that art if they were willing to give their hearts to it and sing in the modern manner; but the modern manner does not please them, only the ancient, for the reasons previously discussed or perhaps for others which might be discussed.

One modern doctor[9] says this: "The duplex long in the perfect mode takes up six tempora; in this, Franco, Petrus de Cruce, and all the others are wrong, since it should really take up nine." This doctor seems to be denouncing not merely the ancients, of whom he names two of great merit, but the moderns as well, since in that remark he says that not merely those two but all the others are wrong. He does not say, "the ancients," but says absolutely, "all the others," and in consequence says that he himself is wrong, since he too is numbered among "all." If all those who err are ignorant, that doctor, who reckons all to be ignorant in his statement, appears to speak with bad manners. Let him take care lest he, in that statement to which I just now replied and in others discussed earlier, commit a greater error. Still, I think that he, like all other doctors, believed himself to be speaking the truth.

The old art, it is clear, must not be considered rude and irrational: first, because the arguments brought against it and some of the additions made to it by the moderns have been shown already to be, respectively, contrary to reason or unnecessary to art; and secondly, because even if the moderns have made good additions to the ancient art, it does not follow that the ancient art, or its inventors and practitioners, are in themselves rude and irrational. Thus, granted that the doctors who have succeeded Boethius, such as the monk Guido and others, have made many good additions to the art of tones and modes which he transmitted to us, the art of Boethius and Boethius himself should not on that account be considered rude and irrational. For he laid the foundations of the art and furnished the principles from which others who follow him have drawn good and useful conclusions, consonant with the art and not contrary to or incompatible with those principles.

If the moderns make many distinctions and use many designations with regard to semibreves, the ancients, as has been mentioned, appear to use more insofar as substance is concerned, whatever might be the case with notational figures. For when the ancients used for the same equal tempus, that is, for the breve in its proper sense, now two unequal semibreves, now three, now four,

9. An otherwise unknown theorist whom Jacques had previously quoted and criticized in Chapters 26 and 27 of Book 7 of his *Speculum* (Bragard, pp. 54–57).

five, six, seven, eight, or nine equal ones, these could be called semibreves
secundae when they used two, because two such were the equivalent of the
breve; semibreves tertiae when they used three, because three such equalled
the breve in value; semibreves quartae when they used four, for a similar reason; semibreves quintae, when five; semibreves sextae, when six; semibreves
septimae, when seven; semibreves octavae, when eight; and (as explained
above) semibreves nonae, when nine.[10] Though they made all these distinctions in semibreves, they never distinguished them in their shape and never
gave them tails, but distinguished them sufficiently from each other by means
of points.

47. A Comparison of the Old Art of Mensurable Music with the New As Regards Liberty and Servitude

The modern art of singing seems to compare with the ancient art as a lady
with a bondwoman or a housemaid, for now the new art appears to be the
mistress, and the old art a servant; the new art reigns, the ancient is exiled. But
is it reasonable that the art which uses perfections should be reduced to subjec-
tion and the art which uses imperfections should dominate, when the master
should be more perfect than the slave?

Again, these arts seem to compare with one another as the Old Law with
the New, except that in this comparison the art of the moderns seems to be in
the position of the Old Law and the old music in that of the New Law. For the
New Law is freer, plainer, more perfect, and easier to fulfill; it contains fewer
precepts and is less burdensome to observe. Wherefore our Lord says in the
Gospel: "My yoke is easy and my burden is light."[11] And St. James in his Epistle: "But he who looks into the perfect law, the law of liberty."[12] But the Old
Law contained many and diverse moral, judicial, and ceremonial precepts
which were difficult to fulfill. Whence St. Peter, in the Acts of the Apostles,
speaking of the Old Law: "Why do you make trial of God by putting a yoke
upon the neck of the disciples which neither our fathers nor we have been able
to bear?"[13]

The teachings of the old law of measured music are few and clear compared
with those of the new. It would take a long time to recount how many rules the
moderns use for their various longs, breves, and semibreves; how many different measures and modes of singing; how many diverse instructions they lay
down for causing imperfections; how many rules they use to distinguish their
types of song. Nor are they completely in agreement about their doctrines. For

10. See Chapter 17 of Book 7 (Bragard, pp. 37–39, where Jacques gives examples from Petrus de
   Cruce and an anonymous composer, illustrating the use of from four to nine semibreves for
   the perfect breve.
11. Matthew 11:30.
12. James 1:25.
13. Acts 15:10.

some of them indicate perfect time in their music with a round circle, because the round form is perfect;[14] while others use three little strokes to indicate it. These three strokes must touch one line and project a little on each side, to distinguish them from the strokes that denote rests. And the prescriber of this rule upbraids those who are unaware of it, counting them as foolish and witless, for here resides great science, and great wisdom (and let these things be positive!).[15] Perfect and imperfect time, moreover, can be distinguished from each other in another way from these, indeed in many other ways, if combined with one another.

To indicate the perfect mode they draw a square enclosing three little strokes; but to indicate the imperfect mode, they draw a square enclosing two little strokes. Others indicate the imperfect by drawing a sign made up of two semicircles. By such a sign they denote both the time and the mode; as one of them says: "They do not know how to denote the one without the other." Others presume to prefix an M for the perfect mode and an N for the imperfect, saying that as O and C are used for variation of tempus, so M and N are used for recognition of the mode. Others, as if reversing matters, understand by O the perfect mode and perfect time, but by C the imperfect mode and imperfect time.

Others say that a circle enclosing three little strokes may be used for the perfect mode and time; but to designate the imperfect mode and time they use a semicircle enclosing two little strokes.

The moderns use these things and many others which the ancients never used, and thus they subject this art to many burdens, so that she who before was free from these burdens now seems a bondwoman in this respect. Whereas, according to Seneca, liberty is one of the greatest goods, whence the poetic saying: "Not for all the gold in the world were liberty well sold." Yet while the old art is free from such burdens, the moderns do not permit her to rule. But since that is not a proper regime where the free man who should be master is subject to him who is not free, the Philosopher, in his *Politics*, greatly disapproves of such government or rule.[16]

48. A COMPARISON OF THE OLD ART OF MENSURABLE MUSIC WITH THE MODERN AS REGARDS STABILITY, AND OF THE OLD MODE OF SINGING WITH THE NEW

One important difference, among others, between perfect and imperfect work is that the perfect work is more stable than the imperfect; for the perfect

14. A number of the symbols described here appear in Philippe de Vitry (Gilbert Reaney, André Gilles, and Jean Maillard, eds., *Philipp de Vitriaco Ars Nova*, Corpus Scriptorum de Musica, no. 8 [Rome, American Institute of Musicology, 1964], p. 27). Strunk's omission of the musical examples that illustrate the symbols is maintained in the present edition.

15. The last phrase, used clearly with ironic intent, is puzzling; perhaps there is some technical philosophic meaning involved.

16. Aristotle, *Politics* 1277B and 1279A.

work has no need of another; its existence does not depend on its being ordered with respect to something else; it has a firm foundation. That art, then, which is the more perfect of the two measured arts, the old and the modern, must be the one which is the more stable. Likewise, as has been mentioned above, we sometimes find certain new doctrines to be unstable. Although at first they are gladly and freely accepted because of their novelty, when they are carefully examined their lack of solid foundations causes them to displease and be rejected, and brings about a return to the more ancient teachings. Would that it were thus with the modern art of measured music and the old!

That the modern teachers are not fully in agreement with respect to the art of measured music in their treatises, is a sign of the instability of their art. For it is written: "Every kingdom divided against itself is laid waste";[17] for if one man oppose the other, how will their kingdom stand? Indeed if division spells evil and instability, then, according to the words of the prophet Hosea, "Their heart is divided; now shall they perish."[18]

Moreover, measured music seeks concord and shuns discord. It does not seek discordant teachers to attain these ends; indeed, all things accord together unto good. Would that it pleased the modern singers that the ancient music and the ancient manner of singing were again brought into use! For, if I may say so, the old art seems more perfect, more rational, more seemly, freer, simpler, and plainer. Have not the moderns rendered music lascivious beyond measure, when originally it was discreet, seemly, simple, masculine, and chaste? For this reason they have offended and continue to offend many judicious persons skilled also in music, just as Timotheus the Milesian offended the Spartans and Laconians, something mentioned in our first book.[19]

Let the judicious take heed and decide what is true. For what purpose have the old music and method of singing and the practice of the old art been banished in favor of the moderns and the modern method of singing? What wrong had they done? Were they banished because of their goodness? But they do not please the satraps, as King Achish said to David: "You are upright and good, but you do not please the satraps."[20]

It is illegal that anyone should be an exile from his country save for sure and just cause, and that he should be cut off from the fellowship of the faithful, as if excommunicated, save by his own fault. I do not deny that the moderns have composed much good and beautiful music, but this is no reason why the ancients should be maligned and banished from the fellowship of singers. For one good thing does not oppose another.

In a certain company in which some able singers and judicious laymen were assembled, and where new motets in the modern manner and some old ones were sung, I observed that even the laymen were better pleased with the

17. Luke 11:17.
18. Hosea 10:2.
19. See Bragard, Liber primus, p. 60.
20. 1 Samuel 29:6.

ancient motets and the ancient manner than with the new. And even if the new manner pleased when it was a novelty, it does so no longer, but begins to displease many. So let the ancient music and the ancient manner of singing be brought back to their native land; let them come back into use; let the rational art flourish once more. It has been in exile, along with its manner of singing; they have been cast out from the fellowship of singers with near violence, but violence should not be perpetual.

Wherein does this lasciviousness in singing so greatly please, this excessive refinement, by which, as some think, the words are lost, the harmony of consonances is diminished, the value of the notes is changed, perfection is brought low, imperfection is exalted, and measure is confused?

In a great company of judicious men, when motets in the modern manner were being sung, I observed that the question was asked, what language such singers were using, whether Hebrew, Greek, Latin, or some other, because what they were saying could not be made out. Thus, although the moderns compose good and beautiful texts for their songs, they waste them by their manner of singing, since they are not understood.

This is what it has seemed needful to say in support of the old art of measured music and in defense of those who practice it. And while I have not found any previous teachers who have written of this matter, may I find successors and helpers who will write of it and will fortify with better arguments what I have touched upon.

INDEX

Note: Numbers in boldface refer to pages where definitions for a term are found, or to the source reading passages themselves.